Lemon.

How the advertising brain turned sour.

Orlando Wood

System1 Group

Just when you are starting to think that books on advertising effectiveness are all rather similar, along comes Orlando's book. The book is itself a perfect illustration of the virtues it extols: entertaining, unpredictable, deep, broad-ranging and beautifully crafted.
A book you will <u>want</u> to read.

Peter Field / Peter Field Consulting

An urgent wake-up call and a simple rallying cry for us all – 'we need to entertain for commercial gain'.
We shouldn't need this rigorous and inspiring analysis to remind us of this humble truth.
But unfortunately, we do. Thank you, Orlando.

Sarah Carter *Global Planning Partner /* adam&eveDDB
and Co-author of How ~~Not~~ to Plan

From the Romans to Brian Eno, and all points in between, I found reading Orlando Wood's new book Lemon enriching and educational. For those of us who work in advertising, Orlando shows what's happening on our watch – a crisis in creativity – and, crucially, he also explains how we should fix the problems of our own making. Everyone involved in commissioning, making and carrying advertisements should read his book, and make better ads as a result.

Karen Fraser MBE *Director /* Credos
and *Head of Strategy /* Advertising Association

Contents.

Foreword.

Janet Hull OBE *Director of Marketing Strategy IPA*

This new addition to the EffWorks portfolio is both erudite and entertaining. It manages to link hard fact to consumer insight, cultural context to creative cues, technology advances to changes in mental patterns. In the consultations with practitioners during its development it has met with widespread enthusiasm and support from all sides of our community.

When we launched Effectiveness Week (EffWeek) three years ago it was against the backdrop of a decade of digital revolution in the advertising and marketing services industry. Our objective was, and still is, to draw on the collective intelligence of thought leaders in the industry, from the marketing, media, research and technology sectors, working in partnership with IPA member agencies, to reflect on day-to-day working practice, and identify issues to address through discussion, debate and R&D which are felt to be holding the industry back from achieving peak performance.

This new thesis from Orlando Wood is an important staging post on that journey. Drawing on the IPA Effectiveness Databank analysis of the growth of digital advertising and the concurrent bias to short-term thinking and execution, it picks up on the findings of Peter Field's summer 2019 call to arms (*The Crisis in Creativity*) and offers a cultural, sociological and neuroscientific explanation for the current creative malaise. It also offers a rich new evidence base that supports an understanding of the problem and its solution,

in the form of proprietary System1 Group research, and a wider 'test and learn' approach to interrogate the opportunity.

Creativity in the service of brands and businesses is our industry point of difference, but, as in every other part of our world, the application of it is being reshaped. The creative conventions of the analogue world do not always translate easily into the digital era. We risk leaving behind some of the timeless principles for generating brand ideas which make creativity great. How do we reinvent them for the internet age? The digital era provides us with new creative technologies, such as richer immersive XR interactive experiences. How do we bring creative ideas to life in a multi-media, multi-platform world? How do we harness them for brand building as well as sales activation?

Lemon challenges the industry to recognise the creative direction it has taken in the digital era and is designed to open a healthy and productive industry debate. At our best, we have an extraordinary ability to innovate, imagine and create advertising works of art that elevate, expand and transform brand and human experience. We know that creativity is the biggest multiplier of marketing effectiveness. Now is the time to transform our creative culture for the digital era, integrating the best of the old with the best of the new. We look forward to a new golden era of creative invention.

Preface.

Orlando Wood *Chief Innovation Officer* System1 Group
Member of the IPA Effectiveness Advisory Board

Advertising is a force for good.

Its primary role is economic. Every £1 spent on it in the UK adds £6 to the country's GDP.[1] It sustains company growth, competitiveness and innovation. It creates employment, and to many more than just the half or so million people in the UK who work in it.

It benefits each of us, because it fuels the growth that leads to better, more affordable products and services.

It provides a cultural benefit, funding the media, arts and sports that we love — costs that people are not willing or able to fund themselves. Without it, some of these cherished things might cease to exist.

And beyond its financial contribution to society, advertising establishes common cultural reference points that bind people together.

But all is not well in adland.

A golden age for advertising technology has not translated into a golden age for advertising. In a period of technological innovation, advertising effectiveness has fallen. Short-termism, specialisation and narrowness of focus are on the rise. And, as this book will show, advertising styles have emerged that are diametrically opposed to effectiveness.

Advertising *creativity* is in crisis.

It is all to do with the way the brain attends to the world: the same instincts that lie behind short-termism and narrow focus are resulting in work that is flat, abstract, dislocated and devitalised – advertising that doesn't *move* people. An attentional shift has occurred in business and society;

a change in thinking style that has left its mark not just on advertising, but on popular culture. We have entered a *creative Reformation*: a new literalness, a drive for 'authenticity', a 'stripping of the altars' that has dangerous consequences for advertising effectiveness.

The focus of this publication is therefore firmly on *what makes ads effective*, because if the ads themselves don't work, the whole advertising ecosystem runs to seed.

This publication is in five sections.

First, we demonstrate the power of advertising creativity; that how advertising makes audiences feel translates into tangible business outcomes. The problem is that advertising is losing its ability to make people feel; creativity is in crisis.

Second, we describe the brain's attentional styles. We will learn how to read these attentional styles in culture over the course of Western civilization. This type of attentional shift has left its mark on culture before.

In section three, we will see how a shift in attentional style has stripped away the very thing that makes advertising work and has replaced it with something that doesn't. Advertising has lost its humanity and its ability to entertain; it has *turned sour*.

In section four, we explore why this change in attentional style is happening in agencies and client companies today, and propose how they might guard against it.

Finally, in section five, we will point towards a more effective advertising style that creates and sustains business growth.

Analysis throughout draws on the IPA Effectiveness Databank and System1 Group's advertising database.

1 Deloitte/Advertising Association, *Advertising Pays* 2013

We are facing a crisis in creativity

Section 1
Setting the scene:
Creativity and Effectiveness

What's happening to advertising effectiveness?

Advertising can change a company's fortunes. It creates and sustains growth by reaching new customers and it improves profitability by reducing price sensitivity towards brands and products.

But advertising effectiveness is falling, and we need to understand why.

For a while, advertising effectiveness had been rising. The early years of the 21st century saw a rise in advertising effectiveness that can be attributed to the benefits of new digital activation. Adding paid search (a widely accessible type of classified advertising) to TV led to a sharp rise in campaign effectiveness. But this period of improving effectiveness has been followed by a gradual decline.

Since 2008, advertisers have begun to spend less than necessary on brand (and more than is desirable on activation) advertising.[2] As Peter Field once put it, "We threw away all the benefits of the digital revolution".[3]

This shift in effectiveness can be explained by a concurrent surge in short-termism, a narrowing of focus. Figure 2 illustrates how the proportion of short-term campaigns in the IPA Effectiveness Databank has risen since 2006.

These shorter campaign periods are an important factor in declining effectiveness. Budget pressures in the wake of the downturn have also led to clients cutting budgets or reallocating them to newer, less expensive online channels, whose measures of effect are geared towards the short term. The trend for companies to do more of their business online has also contributed to this short-term mentality. We know this because short-termism is particularly marked among online brands and categories that rely on high levels of consumer online research.[4]

There is, however, another strand to the story, which is the focus of this volume: we have seen changes to advertising styles in this period that are detrimental to its effectiveness.

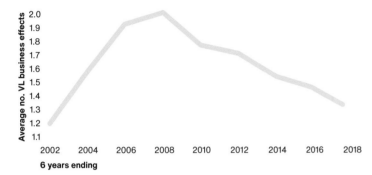

Fig 1 Advertising effectiveness is falling
From *The Crisis in Creative Effectiveness*, IPA, 2019

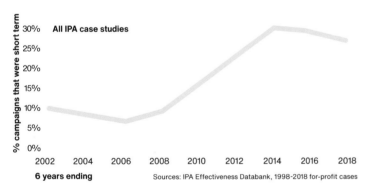

Fig 2 The rise in short-termism
From *The Crisis in Creative Effectiveness*, IPA, 2019

2 See *Effectiveness in Context,* Binet & Field, IPA, 2018, pp 111-113. Peter Field explains that in the early years of digital activation, budget allocation between brand building and activation was maintained close to the optimal 60:40 split
3 Personal correspondence with Peter Field
4 See *Effectiveness in Context,* Binet & Field, IPA, 2018, pp 117-120

Why creativity matters.

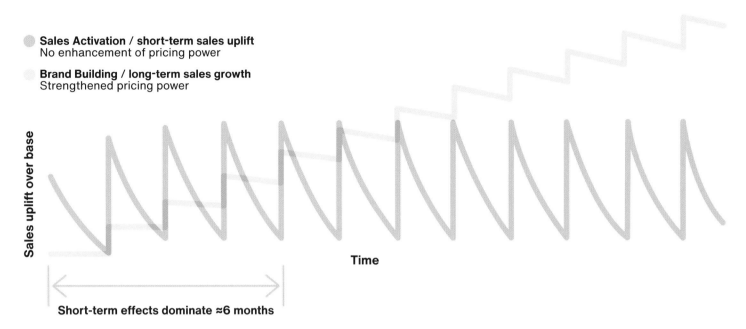

● **Sales Activation / short-term sales uplift**
No enhancement of pricing power

● **Brand Building / long-term sales growth**
Strengthened pricing power

Sales uplift over base

Time

Short-term effects dominate ≈6 months

Fig 3 The contribution of sales activation and brand building advertising over time
From *The Long and the Short of It*, Binet & Field 2013

The IPA have demonstrated that advertising works in two different ways: it can achieve both long-term and short-term effects. Marketing can be broadly categorised into brand-building and sales-activation activities. Binet and Field use the chart above to illustrate how these two marketing activities work differently over time.

The effect of brand-building campaigns is cumulative and takes time to establish, whereas sales-activation effects are episodic and immediate. The big payback comes from long-term sales effects, which prime the consumer to choose the brand through the creation of memory structures and improve profitability through increased 'pricing power'.[5]

Les Binet and Peter Field point to an established marketing principle: that a brand that spends above its size (achieves excess or extra share of voice – ESOV) can expect its market share to **increase** in the subsequent year; a brand that spends below its size (does not have share of voice sufficient for its size) will **decline** in the subsequent year. Binet and Field indicate that on average across all campaigns, 0.5% points of growth are achieved for 10% points of extra share of voice.[6]

Illustrative Example:

If a brand's share of market is 10% and its share of voice is 20%, then its ESOV is 10% (20 minus 10 equals 10).

It stands to grow by 0.5% points as a result over the period.

5 *Effectiveness in Context,* Binet & Field, IPA, 2018
6 See *Marketing in the Era of Accountability*, IPA, 2008, for further details, and newer ESOV-SOM gain guidelines in *Effectiveness in Context,* IPA, 2018

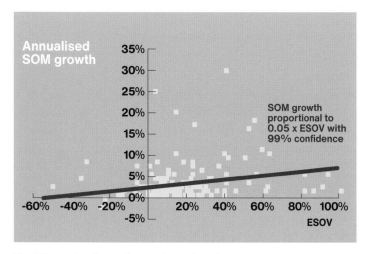

Fig 4 How extra share of voice determines future market-share growth
From *The Long and the Short of it*, Binet & Field, IPA, 2013

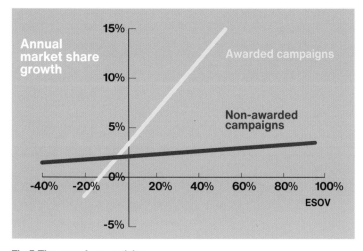

Fig 5 The case for creativity
From *Selling Creativity Short*, IPA, 2016

This relationship gives us a helpful model to assess the effectiveness of campaigns over a longer time period. Campaigns that result in exceptional growth per point of extra share of voice can be described as *effective*.

Peter Field uses this relationship to demonstrate the value of creativity: advertising campaigns in the IPA Effectiveness Databank that win creative awards are more profitable on this basis than those that don't win awards.[7] The Gunn Report documents creative award wins at the world's top 46 creative shows. When this is overlaid on the IPA Effectiveness Databank we see just how valuable creativity is: a 12:1 long-term efficiency advantage for creatively awarded campaigns.

Creatively awarded campaigns can be said to be more effective because the relationship between ESOV and share growth is much stronger for them than non-awarded campaigns. Field's analysis also tells us that creatively awarded campaigns are more likely to employ **emotional strategies** than non-awarded campaigns.

Emotional strategies for the long term.

There is further evidence for emotional strategies helping over the long term. Binet and Field's meta-analysis of the IPA Effectiveness Databank has repeatedly shown the effectiveness of emotional advertising strategies. Campaigns that their authors declare as having an 'emotional' strategy are nearly twice as likely to report very large profit gains over the long term as those that do not, as illustrated below.[8]

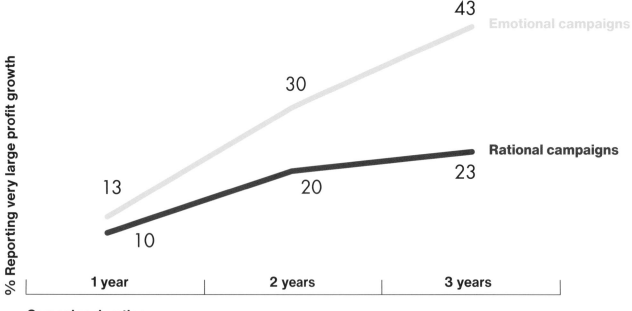

Fig 6 The advantage of emotional strategies over the long-term
From *The Long and the Short of it*, Binet & Field, IPA, 2013

Why emotional strategies work over the long term.

Advances in psychology over the last thirty years leave us in little doubt that people are fast and frugal thinkers when it comes to making everyday decisions, and decide quickly whenever possible, trusting plausible judgements that come easily to mind.[9] Daniel Kahneman proposes that humans have two systems of thought – one fast and easy, the other slow and effortful. System 1 is the fast, intuitive, emotionally guided and automatic mode of thinking and it is intrinsically long term in the way that it operates. For any advertiser wishing to influence long-term growth, it's vital to understand its features.

System 1 learns very gradually over time, through repeated experience, to help us make quick and automatic decisions in the future. Emotional associations are an important feature of System 1, because emotional response helps us to mark our experiences in long-term memory as good, bad or indifferent. This helps us to conjure up a feeling for or against a certain course of action for any related situation in the future. Psychologist and neuroscientist Antonio Damasio calls these memories 'somatic markers', because they are literally imprinted in the flesh (*söma* is Greek for 'body').[10] Feeling happens before thinking ('thinking' is more rooted in language), is evolutionarily older and more strongly associated with motivation.[11]

Another feature of System 1 is that we constantly scan our environment for things we recognise, and reward anything we can process quickly and easily. We are more inclined to choose brands that we can recognise quickly and easily – that have 'processing fluency' – and we also confer greater value on them, as we shall see in Section 5. For System 1, brands that come easily to mind, that feel good and that are easily recognised – that have fame, feeling and fluency – are a good choice. So, a marketer's goal is not to increase consideration, as commonly thought, but to *reduce it*; to make decision-making as quick and intuitive for people as possible.

When it comes to creative development for long-term brand building therefore, it follows that ads need to generate both a positive emotional response and offer up a distinctive hook for the audience.[12] Advertising that achieves this for a brand will, on future occasions, guide us quickly and easily to decide in its favour. Long-term memories are formed through emotional response, so even if we're not in the market for the product today, any emotional associations with the brand that are created by its advertising will stay with us, making the brand more salient to us in the future when we might then be in the market for it.

Campaigns with an 'emotional' strategy are nearly twice as likely to report very large profit gain over the long term as those that do not.

7 *Selling Creativity Short,* IPA, 2016

8 *The Long and the Short of it,* Binet & Field, IPA, 2013

9 *Thinking Fast and Slow,* Kahneman, D., 2012 pp159-160

10 *Descartes' Error*, Damasio, A., Vintage 2006 pp173-196

11 *The Righteous Mind*, Haidt, J.,2013. Haidt references Zajonc's important findings, p66

12 For a longer discussion on the importance of distinctive assets, see *How Brands Grow, Sharp, B., 2010* and *Building Distinctive Brand Assets,* Romaniuk, J., 2018

A human measure of creative effectiveness.

What if we could measure the emotional response audiences felt towards advertising and use this to adjust ESOV to predict long-term growth? If we could establish the actual *emotional response* a viewer feels towards an advert, we could use it to explain its business success.

System1 measures viewers' emotional response to an ad with human, System 1 facial coding.[13] The approach is based on the work of psychologist Paul Ekman and his model of emotion. The seven basic emotions are: happiness, fear, disgust, anger, surprise, contempt and sadness.[14] System1 also features neutrality in its question, because it's perfectly possible that people are left unmoved by an ad. The approach differs from automated facial coding in that rather than relying on an algorithm to interpret how audiences feel, System1 *asks people to indicate how they feel* about an ad shown to them. They select one of the seven basic emotions or neutral from a pictorial scale; an exercise that favours fast and frugal processing. In this way, across a large quantitative sample, it's possible to establish how an ad leaves people feeling – the blend of emotions it elicits.

It's also possible to build up a picture of how people feel during the ad. One of the benefits of the approach, as we will see, is that it is highly replicable and can be deployed at scale.

In a study conducted in 2009, System1 blind tested campaigns for which the IPA Effectiveness Databank held business-effects data. Independent analysis by Peter Field on behalf of the IPA, using the IPA Effectiveness Databank, verified that campaigns generating a greater emotional response in System1's testing achieved a greater number of very large business effects.

Ads that people felt strongly about were more likely to achieve in-market penetration gain, share gain and reductions in price sensitivity. Emotional response to the campaign also predicted market-share growth, once levels of ESOV had been accounted for.[15]

What type of response drives these long and broad effects? Advertising that leaves people feeling good (happy).

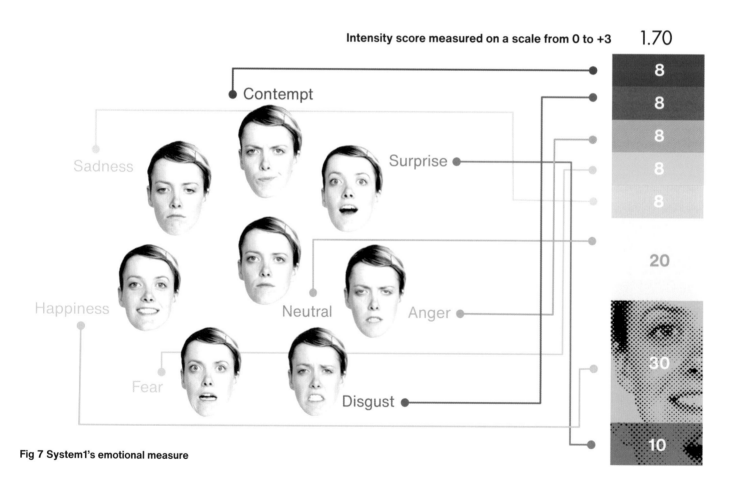

Intensity score measured on a scale from 0 to +3   1.70

Contempt
Sadness
Surprise
Happiness
Neutral
Anger
Fear
Disgust

8
8
8
8
8
20
30
10

Fig 7 System1's emotional measure

13 Note that we use the term 'System 1' throughout to describe the type of thinking referred to by Kahneman and 'System1' to refer to System1 Group plc
14 *Emotions Revealed,* Ekman, P., Phoenix, London 2003
15 For a longer description of the method and experiment, see 'How Emotional Tugs Trump Rational Persuasion', Wood, O., *Journal of Advertising Research* 2012, 52(1), pp31-39
16 *Descartes' Error*, Damasio, A., Vintage 2006, p173

Neutrality, contempt, disgust, anger, fear and sadness are not associated with these long-term effects, though the experiment showed that some of these 'negative' emotions can be elicited to very good effect in storytelling, if successfully resolved by happiness. Positive associations with your brand help to guide the consumer the next time they are buying from your category; they ensure your brand comes to mind first and reduce the salience of other options.[16]

Further testing has enabled us to develop an enhanced 'share of voice to share of market growth' model, which uses emotional response to adjust upwards or downwards the level of growth that might be achieved from share of voice alone. Positive weights are given to happiness and surprise, negative weights to neutrality and the other emotions. Applying positive or negative weights to each emotion enables us to translate the raw emotional profile of advertising into a simple star rating, where 1-Star = weak (no growth amplification likely), through to 5-Star = strongly positive emotional response (strong growth-amplification potential). Highly emotional 5-Star advertising achieves greater growth than 2-Star advertising for the same % point of ESOV. If you want to achieve strong growth, create 3-, 4- or ideally 5-Star emotional work, and ensure you are performing better and spending more than your competitors for your size.

Ads people feel strongly about are more likely to achieve in-market penetration gain, share gain and reductions in price sensitivity.

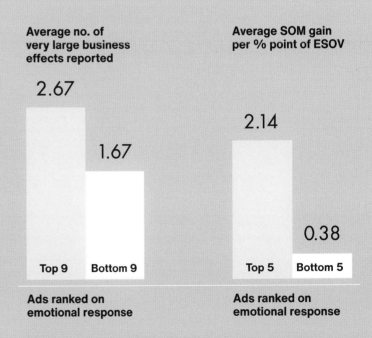

Average no. of very large business effects reported

2.67 — Top 9
1.67 — Bottom 9

Ads ranked on emotional response

Average SOM gain per % point of ESOV

2.14 — Top 5
0.38 — Bottom 5

Ads ranked on emotional response

Fig 8 Overlaying emotional testing on to the IPA Effectiveness Databank allows us to see how emotional response to creative can be used to separate good from great advertising. 18 ads were tested in total, 10 of which reported SOM/ESOV data

The model in practice.

Let's examine how the model works. As a share of voice and market model, it's helpful to establish the emotional response to all advertising in a category. Testing every cereal ad that aired in the UK over the course of a year enables us to determine how predictive the model is of market-share growth (Figure 9, period marked in yellow).

We can establish how well the standard ESOV to SOM growth model performs against actual value market-share changes by comparing IRI market-share data for each brand in the year prior and in the year 6 months on from the start of the advertising measurement period.

We can also run the ESOV to SOM growth model, correcting for emotional response, to see whether the model improves the prediction.

Predicted share gain using the basic ESOV to SOM growth model returns a slight positive correlation with actual value market-share gain, but media spend alone can't account for much of the change in market share. When we use the Star rating to correct for emotional response, however, we markedly improve the basic ESOV to SOM share growth model, enabling it to predict brand share changes over the course of a year for an entire category with high levels of confidence.

UK Cereals category

- **£700m+ annual category value**
- **£24m+ annual TV spend**
- **55 ads represented**

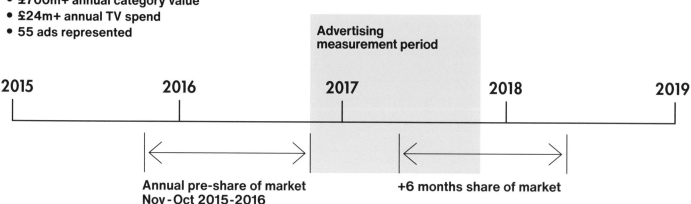

Advertising measurement period

2015   2016   2017   2018   2019

Annual pre-share of market Nov-Oct 2015-2016

+6 months share of market

Fig 9 Predicting share growth for the UK Cereals category
Sources: Ebiquity (TV advertising spend) and IRI (sales data)

Quantity of advertising (TV ESOV)

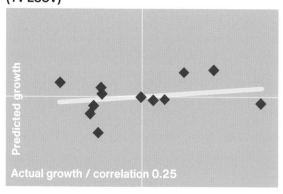

Predicted growth

Actual growth / correlation 0.25

Quantity and quality of advertising (TV ESOV x Star rating)

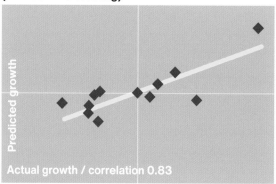

Predicted growth

Actual growth / correlation 0.83

Fig 10 Annual value market-share predictions for the UK Cereal category. Graph above left shows ability of basic ESOV to SOM gain model to predict actual value market-share changes; graph above right shows enhanced emotional ESOV to SOM gain model

The table below demonstrates how the Star rating can be used to correct ESOV to explain share in categories analysed to date. The final two columns show the correlation between 1) the basic ESOV to SOM gain model and market-share growth and 2) the ESOV to SOM gain model *corrected for emotional response* and market-share growth. The time periods and sales data sources are shown; these are determined by the availability of System1's testing data. We use value share wherever possible, because one of the benefits of emotional advertising is its ability to maintain prices.[17]

Whether the categories are short or long purchase cycle, grocery or impulse or so-called 'rational' or 'emotional' categories, the emotional model is a marked improvement on ESOV alone. Taken together these modelled categories account for 411 ads, representing over $826m TV spend, in categories with combined sales of over $48bn.

Category	#Ads tested	#Brands	Value of advertising (12mths of monitoring)	Represented category size (for SOM)	12mths ad monitoring period for SOV/Stars	SOM data source	Correlation with ESOV	Correlation with emotionally amplified ESOV
Cereals UK	55	12	£24.1m	£702m	To Oct (31st) 2017	IRI UK (£)	0.25	0.83
Cereals US	77	15	$289.2m	$7.03bn	To May (31st) 2018	IRI US ($)	0.59	0.74
Gum US	20	6	$83.0m	$3.19bn	To May (31st) 2018	IRI US ($)	0.30	0.67
Savoury Snacks UK	29	15	£25.8m	£1.77bn	To March (31st) 2018	IRI UK (£)	0.49	0.62
Toothpaste US	43	6	$231.7m	$2.86bn	To May (31st) 2018	IRI US ($)	0.50	0.75
Yoghurts UK	33	9	£24.1m	£828m	To March (31st) 2018	IRI UK (£)	0.71	0.82
Cars UK	154	31	£148.6m	2.33m	To Oct (31st) 2017	SMMT (Units)	0.27	0.37

Fig 11 The benefits of an emotionally amplified ESOV to SOM growth model across categories

Testing every ad in a category for emotional response helps to predict changes in brand market share.

17 Even where price information is not available, we see an improved relationship with market share for a model that is corrected for emotional response, as the 'Cars UK' example shows (market share expressed in units). We would anticipate the correction to be more marked still with value-share data.

Creativity and effectiveness today.

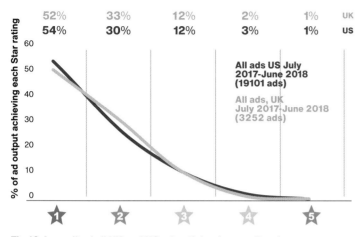

Fig 12 An audit of all UK and US advertising for emotional response
All Automotive, Financial, FMCG, Health & Beauty, Tech and Charity advertising, July 2017 – June 2018, from System1 Ad Ratings database subscription service, www.system1adratings.com

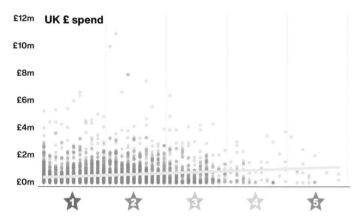

Fig 13 Relationship between Star rating and investment (media spend)
Each point represents an ad (UK). Categories and time period as shown in Fig 12.

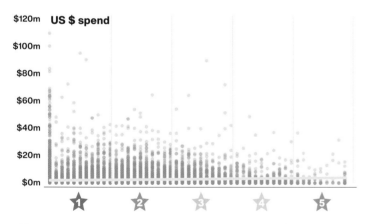

Fig 14 Relationship between Star rating and investment (media spend)
Each point represents an ad (US). Categories and time period as shown in Fig 12.

Testing every ad that airs on TV in this way determines the long-term potential of TV advertising today; it provides a macro picture of advertising performance.

Fig 12 shows the distribution of all TV ads in the US and the UK on System1's Star rating, the share of voice amplifier. Over half of all ads in the UK and US achieve only 1-Star. **Less than half of the ads appearing on TV today are likely to have the emotional impact needed for long-term growth.**

Perhaps spend is greater for the ads with greater long-term growth potential? Figs 13 and 14 show the level of media investment behind each ad. There's little evidence to suggest that advertisers are putting greater spend behind more profitable work. The overall picture is one where investment in the long term – in particular in the US – is little better than random, with vast sums of money being spent on 1- and 2-Star work.

It is not just advertising that appears on TV; the performance of video advertising in digital has a very similar profile. Fig 15 below shows the distribution of a random selection of 100 ads appearing on YouTube compared with UK TV advertising, as shown in Fig 12.

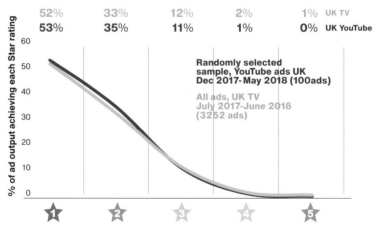

Fig 15 Star rating distribution for UK TV ads vs a random sample of 100 ads from the same categories appearing on YouTube in the six months from Dec 2017 to May 2018

Creatively awarded campaigns and emotional response.

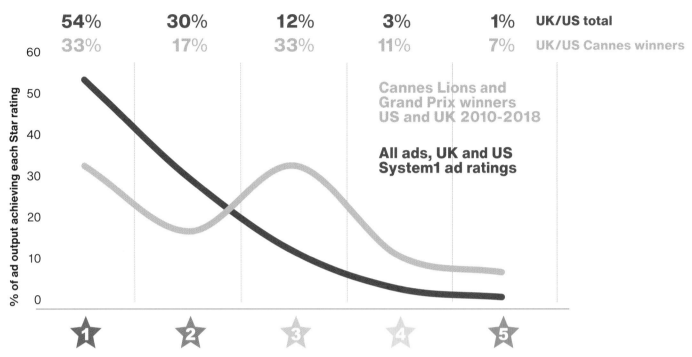

| 54% | 30% | 12% | 3% | 1% | UK/US total |
| 33% | 17% | 33% | 11% | 7% | UK/US Cannes winners |

Cannes Lions and Grand Prix winners US and UK 2010-2018

All ads, UK and US System1 ad ratings

Fig 16 Distribution of US and UK Cannes Grand Prix and Gold Lions winners (2010-2018) vs total ad ratings distribution, US and UK (2017-2018)

Star rating emotional sov amplifier

The IPA's analysis shows that creatively awarded campaigns are more likely to use an emotional strategy, but do they result in a greater emotional response than average? A test of every Cannes Grand Prix and Gold Lions winner in the video category since 2010 shows that they do indeed elicit a stronger emotional response, which helps to explain their increased effectiveness. Ads that win creative awards are **over three times more likely to achieve 3+ Stars than average** (51% vs 16%). Fig16 compares the performance of Cannes winners from 2010-2018 in the UK and US (comparable markets with System1 Ad Ratings) vs the total System1 Ad Ratings market performance, i.e. the market average.

Less than half of all ads achieve the levels of emotional response required to deliver long-term growth.

A crisis in creativity.

Advertising that makes audiences feel good generates market-share growth over the long term. But examples of it are rare, and a pattern is emerging that gives cause for concern. In a new analysis in 2019, shown in Fig 17, Field reports that the creative multiplier ratio for the most creatively respected advertising in the industry has fallen from over 12:1 to just 3:1. The share gain per point of ESOV effectiveness advantage previously enjoyed by creatively awarded campaigns has weakened markedly over time.

Even the most creatively awarded campaigns are not delivering the long-term effects they once did. There are several explanations for this. First, advertisers are focusing more on narrow targeting and short-term effects, so creative focus is being diverted away from brand building towards activation campaigns. Second, more awards are being given to short-term campaigns. There has been a shift towards, as Field puts it, "disposable creativity" and the decline in long-term effectiveness is starting to show.[18]

The problem is bigger than campaign timeframe and budget allocation, however. Fig 18 shows the Star performance of creatively awarded campaigns in System1's testing. It shows that **there has been a rapid decline in the quality of the work itself**. It no longer generates a lasting emotional impression. Creatively awarded advertising is working less and less well with its audience – the general public.

More worryingly, in 2019, the average score for Cannes winners has fallen to its lowest ever level, at 1.6-Stars – **below the typical TV ad**. Creatively awarded campaigns have always been more profitable and performed better among the public than non-creatively awarded campaigns. But no longer.

We are facing a crisis in creativity.

So how do we go about creating work that moves people? To understand this, we need to examine how the brain attends to the world, a subject we will address in the next section.

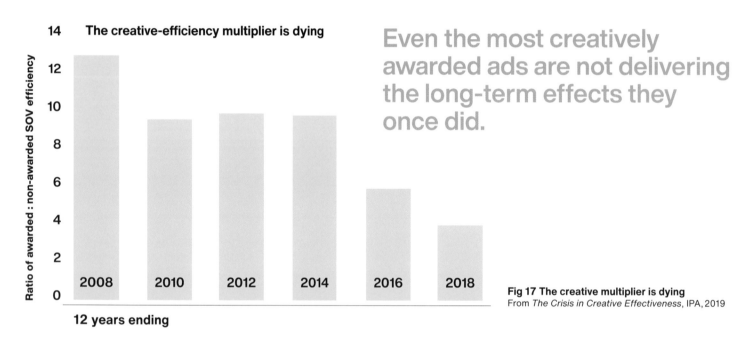

Fig 17 The creative multiplier is dying
From *The Crisis in Creative Effectiveness*, IPA, 2019

> Even the most creatively awarded ads are not delivering the long-term effects they once did.

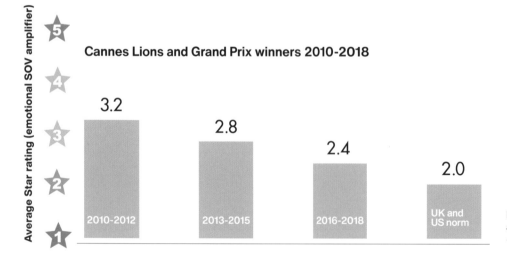

Fig 18 The decline in the performance of UK and US Cannes Lions and Grand Prix winners
46 ads from 2010-2018

Section 1
Summary.

1 Advertising works in two ways, the most important of which brings cumulative long-term growth and is achieved through emotional brand-building advertising.

2 Advertising effectiveness is falling; short-termism and changes in the media landscape are both partly responsible.

3 We can judge the effectiveness of a campaign over the long term by examining the relationship between ESOV and SOM gain; the stronger the relationship the more effective the campaign.

4 Creativity is critical for effectiveness. Creatively awarded campaigns perform better on this long-term measure of growth.

5 Creatively awarded campaigns are more likely to follow an emotional strategy and perform strongly on emotional response measures. A System1 emotional audit of Cannes Lions and Grand Prix winners reveals their emotional advantage.

6 Measuring emotional response to all ads in a category allows an adjustment to ESOV to be made that gives a clearer prediction of brand growth for brands in a category.

7 An audit of TV advertising today in the UK and the US reveals that less than half of all ads achieve the levels of emotional response required to deliver long-term growth, and investment by companies in ads that will work over the long term is little better than random. Emotional response to digital video advertising is remarkably similar.

8 The effectiveness advantage that creatively awarded campaigns enjoy has fallen over the last twenty years. Emotional response to Cannes Lions and Grand Prix winners also reveals how their emotional impact has declined since 2010. They are now no better than the average TV ad.

9 We are facing a crisis in creativity.

The two hemispheres have
different takes on the world and
attend to it differently

Where science meets culture: Creativity and the Brain

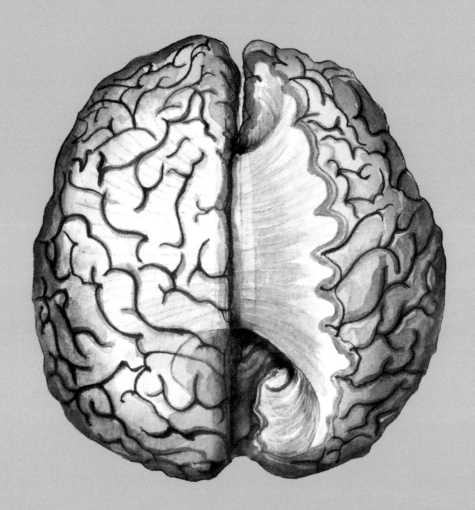

1

The divided brain

With the right brain peeled back to reveal
the *corpus collosum*.

The divided brain.

That the two halves of the brain might do different things was first posited in the 1960s. The idea that one hemisphere 'does reason' and the other 'does emotion', that one is 'analytical' while the other is 'creative' was quick to take hold in popular culture. Sadly, this pop psychology narrative hindered the serious study of brain lateralisation in subsequent years, and the idea that the two halves of the brain might operate differently soon became highly stigmatised as an academic research subject among neuroscientists. But pioneering and painstakingly referenced work by Dr Iain McGilchrist, which we take as a primary source throughout on brain lateralisation, reveals a new and highly nuanced perspective on the brain and how it attends to the world. His thesis is highly pertinent to the febrile world of today, to popular culture and to advertising.[19]

The brain is asymmetrical and it is divided. Its two hemispheres are very different. The right hemisphere is longer, wider and heavier than the left, and they differ in the number and size of neurones, and the number of connective branches put out by each nerve cell. There is greater overlap of these branches in the right hemisphere, which has a greater ratio of white to grey matter than the left. White matter (myelin) enables faster interconnectivity and the right brain's structure means that transfer *across* regions is easier. In the left hemisphere, by contrast, it is transfer of

It's not that they *do* different things, it's more that they do things *differently.*

information *within* localised brain regions that is prioritised. The two hemispheres also differ in their sensitivity to hormones, pharmacological agents and depend on different neurotransmitters (dopamine left, noradrenaline right).[20]

Not only do the two hemispheres differ structurally, but they remain to this day divided. The only bridge between them is the *corpus callosum*: a bundle of fibres that connects similar regions in each hemisphere. Yet only 2% of all cortical neurones are connected by it.[21] Whilst the *corpus callosum* bridges and connects, its primary function is in fact to allow one hemisphere to inhibit the other, and as McGilchrist asserts, it's getting proportionally smaller over human history and functionally more inhibitory.[22] Information transfer is slower from left to right hemisphere than from right to left, and the suppressive effect of the left hemisphere on the right is greater than that of the right on the left.[23]

McGilchrist's study of split-brain experiments and observation of patients with damaged brain hemispheres reveals that left and right hemispheres are not only structurally different, but that they attend to the world differently. It's not that they *do* different things, as we used to think; it's more that they do things *differently*. They have different takes on the world, different attentional styles.

19 See *The Master and His Emissary*, Iain McGilchrist 2019
20 Idem. p33
21 Idem. p17
22 Idem. pxx (20), preface to the new edition
23 Idem. p218

Types of attention.

In humans, as in other mammals, and birds, it transpires, the left brain brings a very narrow focus to bear on the world, whereas the right brain attends to the world in a much broader sense. It's instructive to consider how this works in birds because it helps to establish some important principles. In birds, the left hemisphere, controlling the right eye, looks for grains of food on the ground by abstracting them from their context and categorising them, thus allowing it to identify the food and what to pick up. The right hemisphere meanwhile, controlling the left eye, is attentive to the broader context around, is vigilant and scans the environment for threats and predators.[24]

Psychologists broadly point to five types of attention: vigilance, sustained attention, alertness, focused attention and divided attention. McGilchrist asserts that of these five types of attention, only *focused* attention is exclusively taken care of by the left brain; the others principally rely on the right hemisphere.[25] The right hemisphere is constantly 'on the lookout' for what might be interesting or new, for what might stand out, and is necessarily very comfortable with novelty, contradiction and ambiguity. The left hemisphere then latches on to what the right hemisphere sees. The right brain presents the world to us as it is; the left brain represents it for us, abstracting it from its context, flattening what it sees, seeing only the parts, reducing it to a symbol. Illustrations 2 and 3 opposite, are taken from a study that reveals how each hemisphere sees the world.[26]

The participants were asked to draw a flower and the function of one or other of their brain hemispheres was suppressed by *unilateral electroconvulsive seizure*. In Illustration 2, each row is drawn by a different person; each column shows how the flower is drawn when both hemispheres are active, or when one or other hemisphere only is active. When both hemispheres are active, the flower is rendered as a whole and in some detail. When the right hemisphere only is active, the whole flower is depicted, with stem, leaves and flowerhead, and though it lacks a little detail, it is represented fully and in three dimensions. When the left brain draws the flower, however, it is abstracted and flattened, a mere representation of a flower – a detailed but prototypical symbol that *denotes* a flower.

We need both hemispheres to see the world as it really is.

When left to its own devices, the left brain sees the world as flat, abstracted and devitalised, as the drawings of familiar items by the left brain (Illustration 3) show.

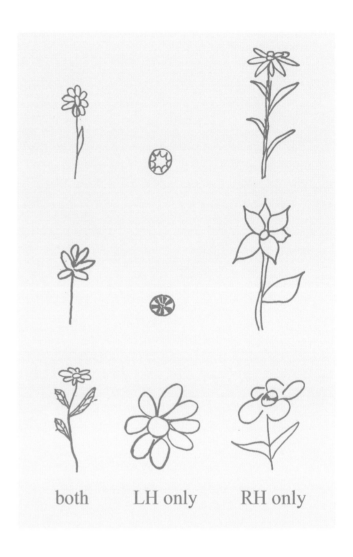

both   LH only   RH only

2
Above
Drawing of a flower

Conducted by participants' whole brain (both), left hemisphere only (LH) and right hemisphere (RH).

3
Opposite
Drawings of everyday objects

According to the left hemisphere (when the right brain is inactivated).

24 For a detailed description of hemispheric attention in birds and mammals, see *The Master and His Emissary*, pp25-28
25 Idem. pp38-39
26 'Representation activity of the right and left hemispheres of the brain', Nikolaenko, N. N., Egorov, A. Y. & Freiman, A. E., *Behavioural Neurology* 1997, 10(1), pp49-59

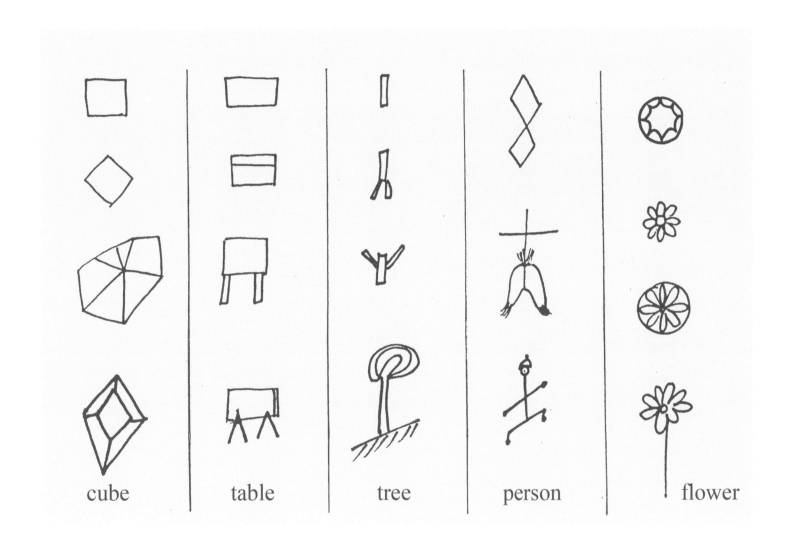

cube   table   tree   person   flower

When left to its own devices,
the left brain sees the world as flat,
abstracted and devitalised

The left brain grasps (with the right hand), and has a narrower and more goal-oriented focus. Its tendency is to isolate parts from the whole and to see them in the abstract. It creates an internally consistent representation of the world but can only build up its picture from the parts and is reliant on what the right brain feeds it. It likes to break things up into smaller parts, to categorise, and therefore favours the familiar, consistency, repeatability and predictability.

The left brain prefers to see things in terms of simple and linear cause and effect. It prizes utility, power and control, and its ability to abstract and isolate things from their context enables it to manipulate the world. It creates and uses models and tools for this purpose; it likes to make things and likes what it makes. Its principal tool is language, which resides largely in the left hemisphere (though important aspects of language are also processed by the right brain) and has a predilection for symbols and signs. It favours clarity and certainty, and is very literal, preferring things to be explicit. It cannot deal with contradiction or ambiguity, seeing things as either categorical lies or truths. It is rather controlling and dogmatic, and it is notable that, of all the emotions, it is anger that lateralises to the left (anger is motivated by a sense of losing control). Its model of the world is flat and simplified, lacking in depth or nuance.

The left brain wilfully ignores or cuts off anything outside its model of the world, which means it lives in a rigid, fixed and self-referential hall of mirrors, with an often unfounded sense of optimism. It has a very poor grasp of autobiographical detail and little appreciation of its place in time, with no sense of flow. Rather, it sees the world as a series of moments or snapshots, and it lives firmly in the present or its planned future. It controls language but has little gift for music, unable to appreciate anything much beyond simple rhythm. It cannot appreciate and undermines beauty. It has a poor perception of depth and, left to its own devices, wilfully ignores anything in the left visual plane. The left brain is rather self-conscious, bordering on the paranoid, and has very little sense of responsibility for its actions or a sense of guilt in relation to its behaviour towards others or society as a whole.

Characteristics of the left brain.

The right brain, on the other hand, sees the whole rather than the parts. Its attention is broad. It has a highly interconnected structure and, rather than seeing cause and effect, it understands the world through the relationships and connections between things. It is firmly rooted in bodily or visceral experience, and whereas the left brain has a predilection for things, the right brain understands the *living*.

The right brain is empathetic, understands the feelings of others in their faces, gestures and expressions, and understands what is *implied*. It is acutely aware of the space, distance and connection between people – what might be described as 'betweenness'. It attends to what's novel and so has the flexibility to cope with apparent contradiction. It can, for instance, understand how it might be possible to find a certain kind of joy in melancholy.

The right brain's ability to hold two competing thoughts at once also enables it to understand and use metaphor, humour and irony. If the left brain uses language as a tool, the right brain has a more sophisticated sense of what it actually means, plays with it, and happily introduces contradiction and ambiguity to hint at another level of understanding. Poetry and idiom are therefore highly reliant on the right brain. It understands the passing of time ('lived time') and has a sense of flow — of events unfolding in time. It has a natural affinity with the past and is predisposed to nostalgia and sadness. If the left brain 'wants', the right brain 'yearns'; if the left brain 'grasps', the right brain 'explores'.

If language principally resides in the left hemisphere, music is the natural language of the right, because it's the right's ability to see the whole, perceive depth and appreciate the passing of time that also enables it to enjoy melody, timbre, counterpoint and harmony (harmony is the aural equivalent of visual depth), and music in the minor key. The right brain is self-aware and sees the world how it really is. It also has a moral sense, a sense of duty, responsibility and therefore guilt.[27]

27 For further reading on the pro- and anti-social tendencies of the left and right brain, see 'Cerebral Lateralization of Pro- and Anti-Social Tendencies', Hecht, D., in *Experimental Neurobiology* March 2014, 23(1), pp1-27

Characteristics of the right brain.

Hemispheric balance and imbalance.

McGilchrist describes how many mental-health problems can in some part be attributed to hemispheric imbalance and an impairment of right-brain function. Schizophrenia has at its core hyperconsciousness (schizophrenics will often portray an all-seeing eye watching over them in their drawings) and a disturbance in a person's ability to relate to the physical world. Aside from an unbearable sense of anxiety, schizophrenics feel 'emptied of emotion', and shocking or painful ideas can be welcomed to relieve their state of detachment and isolation. Distortions in a person's sense of their body image – reliant on the right parietal lobe – manifest themselves in self-harm and conditions such as *anorexia nervosa*. Both anorexia and self-harm are associated with feeling cut off from one's feelings and embodied existence. Autism and Asperger's syndrome are also marked by clinical features associated with left-brain dominance.[28]

Left-brain dominance can be found not just in those with mental-health problems, however. Left-brain dominance occurs in individuals and across groups – in companies, international corporations and even entire populations.

The intersection between psychology and anthropology is an important development in psychology. It enables us to consider how the mind works in its cultural surroundings. As cultural psychologist Jonathan Haidt puts it

"You can't study the human mind while ignoring culture, as psychologists usually do, because minds function only once they've been filled out by culture. And you can't study culture while ignoring psychology, as anthropologists usually do, because social practices and institutions [...] are to some extent shaped by concepts and desires rooted deep within the human mind, which explains why they often take similar forms on different continents."[29]

McGilchrist describes how at different times in history there has been hemispheric balance and imbalance across populations. As certain modes of thinking begin to dominate, the presence or absence of stimulation in each hemisphere strengthens or eliminates synaptic contacts in the brain, shaping an individual's nervous system, both structurally and functionally. Ways of thinking are imitated and so gradually re-enforced across a population. When there is hemispheric balance, humanity and creativity tend to flourish. But the left brain tends to overreach itself from time to time and shifts towards left-brain dominance can occur to the detriment of society and culture. The self-referential nature of the left brain makes it difficult for it to see any other point of view, so groupthink, orthodoxy and dogma set in. Left-brain attention has undoubtedly moved business and scientific inquiry forward, but for all its brilliance, a dominant left-brain mode of operating is also very limiting and causes many societal difficulties.

Attention is a two-way street; the way we attend to the world influences our interpretation of it, but it also changes the world. At different times in human history, it is possible to discern periods of hemispheric balance and imbalance, because they are manifested in the physical world – in art, sculpture, architecture, music and literature – and in outlook, ways of working and even philosophy. The rest of this section reflects on these changes, because they shed light on what is happening in Western society[30] – and to advertising – today. As we shall come on to describe, we have entered a period of left-brain dominance.

What follows cannot claim to be a comprehensive history of Western culture, of course. Its purpose is to highlight what left- and right-brained takes on creativity look and feel like, and how they relate to the spirit of the age in which they were created. This might at first seem like a digression, but it is important to learn how the left and right brain manifests itself in culture, so that when, in the next section, we start to look at the features of advertising, we can explore how advertising has changed.

The analysis rests on McGilchrist's masterful cultural analysis but also draws on many other sources where helpful.

28 *The Master and His Emissary*, pp395-398 and 403-307
29 *The Righteous Mind*, pp115-116
30 Western culture remains a dominant influence on advertising and we hope it will therefore be of great interest and applicability beyond those living in the West.

From the Roman Empire to the Middle Ages.

The second half of the third century A.D. was a troubled period for the Roman Empire. Pressure and invasions came from nearly every frontier, civil wars broke out across the Empire, and Emperors were continually murdered and usurped. It was against this backdrop that Emperor Diocletian came to power. Diocletian assumed divine sovereignty, without the traditional approval from the Senate, and set about the establishment of the Tetrarchy, with an Emperor in the East and in the West, and a Caesar by each of their sides. People's everyday lives changed dramatically, and "the free and natural forms of the early Empire, the multiplicity and variation of life under a decentralised administration, was replaced by homogeneity and uniformity under an ever-present and increasingly more centralised hierarchy of civil officials".[31]

The average person's life also changed dramatically: each was given a role in society, and made responsible for military and financial duties, such as tax collection. The administration of state was organised into military categories. Freedom to work was replaced by *an obligation to work for the state*. Free guilds were organised into corporations: corn merchants and ship owners now had to supply provisions for Rome. *Standardisation and centralisation* were imposed on the Empire, and an equalisation of Roman provinces occurred that resulted in Italy losing its pre-eminence. To counter rising inflation, Diocletian introduced a price law, fixing and standardising prices across the Empire. Non-adherence meant the death penalty. Unable to make a profit, people closed their businesses, but Diocletian introduced a law to counter this, ensuring that a son had to continue the business of his father. The result of all of this was a rigid and fixed order where people were bound to their specialised professions.[32]

As McGilchrist points out, these moves towards standardisation, centralisation and categorisation are the preferred working style of the left brain. This was a period of left-brain dominance.

Within a few generations, the effect on Roman art, sculpture and architecture was dramatic. Where buildings had used to have an 'organic corporality' – that's to say each part clearly articulated its function – a new emphasis was placed on vast expanses of plain and simple walls. Much like today, there was a new focus on the interior, on the space and light within buildings. Street patterns were ordered and symmetrised. The natural, organic and human forms that had characterised earlier periods in art quickly gave way to a flat, abstracted and devitalised portrayal of people. In sculpture, naturalistic busts that caught human expressions and glances, almost like three-dimensional photographs, became lifeless and symmetrical (see illustrations 4 and 5). Where homes in earlier periods had been decorated with artwork demonstrating a mastery of perspective, now flatness and abstraction emerged (see illustrations 8 and 9). Symbols and lettering started to come to the fore (see illustrations 7, 11 and 13). Where mosaics had once depicted human betweenness and depth, people in *movement*, a new flatness, fixity and devitalisation became manifest (see illustrations 12 and 13).

This flatness and devitalisation in art, reliefs and sculpture would last in Europe for a thousand years until the Renaissance.

31 *Art Forms and Civic Life in the Late Roman Empire*, p3
32 For a fuller account of this fascinating period and its effect on culture, see *Art Forms and Civic Life in the Late Roman Empire*, H.P. L'Orange, which I take as my primary source and summarise here.

4
Top left
Bust of Decius
A.D. 249-251

5
Top right
Bust from the Late Tetrarchy
A.D. 323-337

Note how Decius is caught in a moment; he turns his head and glances upwards. Note the folds in his skin, the naturalistic portrayal of his stubble and tunic. It invites the questions – 'what was going through his mind?', 'what was he reacting to?' Note how the later bust is devitalised and more symmetrical; a blank, expressionless face and eyes. It's more like a death mask than an evocation of the living.

6
Above left
Spiral Tendrils, Ara Pacis Augustae, Rome 9 B.C.

7
Above right
Early Medieval Spiral Tendrils, Santa Sabina, Rome

Note the depth of the tendrils on the Ara Pacis, and the free-flowing and asymmetrical depiction of nature, and how this gives way to a flattened, lifeless, highly uniform and symmetrical pattern in 7. The tendrils lose their naturalistic form and instead become symbolic of the vine, enclosing a further symbol of the cross.

8
Opposite top
Oplontis, Villa of Poppaei Oecus 15, East wall

Note the perspective in the receding columns, the light and shade giving three-dimensional form to the columns in the foreground. The walls are reminiscent of a theatre set depicting a specific time and place. They give a sense of depth to the room.

9
Opposite bottom
Roman Villa at Lullingstone, painted walls, 4th century A.D. British Museum

The colour palette is the same but the style is drastically different. Note the flatness of the columns, the flat and devitalised faces (each priest separated from the other), the symbolism of the crosses, the repeated motif of the priests at prayer and the abstracted decoration throughout and beneath.

10
Opposite top
Procession of Figures
Ara Pacis, Rome 9 B.C.

Note the natural and organic
composition of the characters,
caught in a moment, the sense
of betweenness in community
and how their glances meet.

11
Opposite bottom
Procession of Figures
Saint'Apollinaire, Ravenna
6th century A.D.

Note the repetition and uniformity
of the saints, equal in height, the
flat and devitalised faces, varied
only in their detail, each holding
the symbolic wreath of
martyrdom. Each is separate from
the other – there is no sense of
betweenness. Note also the
intrusion of the words and letters,
and the symbolic halos and palms
of victory behind.

12
Top
Scene from New Comedy
(street musicians), mosaic
Pompeii
late 2nd century, beginning
of 1st century B.C.

13
Above
The Image of Christ, mosaic,
Hinton St Mary, Dorset, British
Museum, 4th century A.D.
The Greek letters X and P indicate
this is probably Christ.

Note the depth and sense of
perspective in the street scene,
how these characters are caught
in a moment, the sense of
betweenness, the light and shade.
This gives way to an altogether
flatter style following the
Tetrarchy, the incursion of symbols
and the flat, expressionless face
that stares blankly out at us.

From the Renaissance to the Reformation.

Florence was the cradle of the Renaissance. After a period of famine and unrest, and the Black Death, the city became very wealthy because it was the home of the Papal bankers, the Medici family, who supported and celebrated the arts and architecture. Civility and service to the community became important social qualities, and it was thought these could only be obtained by the teaching of the humanities. Latin and Greek, grammar, style, rhetoric, literature, moral philosophy and history were therefore taught by what would become known as the Humanists.

The Humanists were aware of their time and place in history. Artwork had gained weight with Giotto, but now it suddenly gained depth too, and this can be dated quite precisely to the year 1425 when Ghiberti won a competition to design a second set of doors for the Florence Baptistry.[33] Perspective and depth – the ability to see things from a distinct time and place – fosters empathy because it puts you in another person's shoes. As McGilchrist puts it, perspective "mediates a view of the world from an individual standpoint – one particular place, at one particular time, rather than a God's-eye view-from-nowhere".[34] Art in this period takes on a new realism, portrays human betweenness and references antiquity.

14
Opposite top
**Bishop Blessing the Fair
at Lendit near St Denis**
Medieval manuscript

15
Opposite bottom
The Renaissance
**Adoration of the Shepherds,
Domenico Ghirlandaio 1485**

Note in the Medieval manuscript, how there is no sense of perspective and that the position and size of the figures is not naturalistic but a means of representing their importance. It looks very much like an organogram from today. The Adoration of the Shepherds is painted with depth and perspective, and contains many references to art and history beyond itself: antiquity in the architectural columns behind and the crib (a Roman sarcophagus); the group of shepherds on the right are a reference to Van de Goes' Nativity in 1475, and in a knowing reference, the shepherd pointing to Christ is Ghirlandaio himself.[35]

33 See 'Italian Art from Masaccio to Mannerism, A New Vision', Murray, P., in *The Age of the Renaissance*, Thames and Hudson, London 1967
34 *The Master and His Emissary*, p300
35 See 'Art and Artists in Northern Europe, The North Transformed', Ettinger, L.D. in *The Age of the Renaissance*, Thames and Hudson, London 1967

16
Opposite
Raphael's The Marriage of the Virgin 1504

Note the masterful perspective and the misty hills receding into the distance. The sense of betweenness and the naturalistic group composition, a group caught in a (historical) moment in time.

17
Above
Allegory of the Old and New Testaments
Hans Holbein the Younger 1530

Note the slightly distorted sense of scale and perspective, and how the painting is compartmentalised into distinct scenes depicting ideas – man, death, salvation, sin and (top left) the law of the Old Testament. Words obtrude on the painting and there is a clear demarcation between the unforgiving Old Testament law (Left) and the New Testament and the path to salvation (Right).

36 The *Master and His Emissary*, p 319
37 *The Master and His Emissary*, p 321
38 McGilchrist refers us to *The Reformation of the Image*, J. L. Koerner, 2009

The Renaissance moved north, but its depth, humanity and exuberance would give way in Northern Europe to a new flatness and devitalisation with the advent of the *Reformation*. A desire for authenticity, which many of us would recognise today, meant that art and spirituality were stripped from churches. Statues that were previously seen as metaphors for the divine – a right-brained 'sense' that one was, before them, in the presence of the divine – gave way to a literal belief that people were worshipping them in their own right. This literal take on 'the statue' led to their removal from churches and their decapitation in public squares. The Gutenberg printing press in the previous century enabled copies of The Bible to be made in German, and 'The Word of God' acquired a new status. The letters VDMA (*Verbum Domini Manet in Aeternum*, The Word of the Lord Endures Forever) were soon to be found on everything from church doors, to helmets and canons. Order was introduced in churches; congregations no longer stood but sat in fixed, regimented pews, facing the front, with the focus no longer on the altar but the pulpit. The Calvinists sought to banish the past and wipe memories of what had been, the left brain thereby removing the "potential for the right hemisphere to have influence through what is implicit and contextual".[36] Pre-*Reformation* art was removed from churches and words of instruction started to obtrude in the new paintings that replaced it. Art became the 'purpose advertising' of its day, a tool to inform and influence the populace. Protestantism ushered in materialism, because it was a way of signalling "spiritual prowess, the reward of God to his faithful".[37] The search for the authentic had stripped from religion the very thing that had imbued it with its spirituality.[38]

18
**The Confession of Augsburg,
Andreas Herneisen 1530**

Note how the painting is broken up
into individual scenes, with no overall
sense of the whole. The whole painting
serves to illustrate the words, which
obtrude upon the scene. As Koerner
points out, the choir master (bottom
right) isn't holding up music but a
biblical command requiring the
choristers to sing – it is a representation
of (not the act of) worship. In this
period, he states, "ideas about the
thing, not the thing itself" dominate.

19
Opposite top
Augsburg Confession
Anonymous 1590
St Johanneskirche, Schweinfurt

The same subject but the style is even more marked than in Illustration 18. Note the distorted perspective, the lack of depth and how the word obtrudes. Note again how the painting is broken up into individual scenes, with no coherent sense of the whole. Note how, as in the Middle Ages, the characters are not in naturalistic proportion to one another; their size is used to convey power and importance.

20
Opposite bottom
Sachs portraited by Herneisen,
Andreas Herneisen 1574

Note the flatness and distorted perspective of the painting, and the awkwardness of the bodily poses, which seems to have a direct line to the modernism of Picasso (cf. Illustration 30). Note also the prominence of the words, the artist's tools laid out on the table, and the repetition of Sachs' image – the representation of Sachs (rather than the man himself) the focal point of the painting.

21
Top left
King Henry VII and his sons
with partner painting

22
Top right
Queen and her daughters,
Flemish School, 16th century,
Syon Park

The painting is symbolic rather than naturalistic, because the king's son, Edmund, and daughters, Elizabeth and Katherine, all died before the age of four (Katherine and her mother Elizabeth died in childbirth in 1503). Note the uniform visual repetition of the figures, differing only in the minutest of detail, disappearing into infinite regress. Each male and each female face shares the same devitalised facial features. Each figure exists in isolation and there is no sense of betweenness. The red rose and other left-brain symbols of state are clearly shown.

23
Above
Coin of Friedrich the Wise 1522
with inscription
Verbum domini manet aeternum

'The Word of the Lord Endures Forever'. McGilchrist references Koerner: "in this period, words acquired the status of things by their aggressive material inscription".[39]

39 The *Master and His Emissary*, p318

From the Baroque to Classicism.

The Baroque period lasted approximately from 1600 to 1750.
A right-brained sensuality and urgency of expression imbued culture of the period. As French philosopher Mme de Chatelet put it, "We have nothing else to do in the world but seek pleasant sensations and feelings", a sentiment that characterised the first half of the 18th century.[40] The period also brought a new period of collaboration between artists and architects (see Illustration 25). Paintings resembling theatrical backdrops now adorned the houses and palaces of the aristocracy; this was the period in which many of the great European palaces and St. Peter's in Rome, with its enormous piazza (Bernini), were built.[41] The effect of this new architecture was one of awe. Fluid motifs and decoration adorned the churches of the period, and rolling, organic and curvilinear forms made their way into architecture. Caravaggio painted scenes of violent movement, with contrasting light and shade; in Canaletto we see depth and ephemeral light effects (see Illustration 24).

Music became an important part of courtly life and the aristocracy commissioned composers such as Monteverdi, JS Bach, Scarlatti and Handel to compose and perform work for them. The bass patterns of dance music helped to develop a sense of key; harmony and cadence developed.[42] Polyphony – multiple individual voices coalescing to form a whole – had appeared in Renaissance music but was now taken to more sophisticated lengths with emphasis on different timbres and contrasts: "loud and soft, fast and slow, high and low".[43] Music thus acquired a drama and tension,

and it sought to sustain emotion in new large orchestral and choral works, such as the *Passions*. Some of the finest examples can be heard in the music of Bach, who shows in his mastery of counterpoint how music can be both appreciated for its individual voices but also as a right-brained whole. It rarely sounds the same on any given hearing, which makes it infinitely fascinating for the right brain, as neurological studies have shown.[44] As McGilchrist puts it, "In harmony as elsewhere, a relationship between expectation and delay in fulfilment is at the core of great art; the art is in getting the balance right, something which Bach consummately exemplifies".[45]

Bach's creative genius was undoubtedly a product of his right-brained, broad attention, and his ability to see the whole as well as the parts. As the quantity and consistency of his output attests, he worked extremely hard, putting himself into his craft and in the way of other composers' music, absorbing these many influences to arrive at his own unique style. He walked 260 miles to see Buxtehude perform, referred to Vivaldi in his concertos and wrote works for the keyboard in the French, English and Italian styles. His Italian influences included Albinoni, Frescobaldi and Bonporti (it was the latter's *Invenzioni* (1712) that most likely inspired Bach's own *Two- and Three-part Inventions* in the 1720s), but he was also influenced by French composers Dieupart and Grigny.[46] We will return to this magpie tendency when we discuss advertising development in section 4.

Listening note 1
The heart-wrenching, restless and anxious opening chorus of the *St. John Passion*, BWV 245. McGilchrist describes Bach's music as having "wonderful passing dissonances and false relations [that] are introduced to be resolved".[47]

Listening note 2
Erbarme dich, mein Gott, um meiner Zähren Willen! ('Have mercy Lord, My God, for the sake of my tears') from the *St Matthew Passion*, BWV 244,[48] which depicts Peter's lament in the garden after having denied knowing Jesus three times. The work evokes profound sadness and a complex array of emotions that defy literal description or explanation.

Listening note 3
The intricate and falling cadences of the *Fugue in A minor* for organ, BWV 543, to be appreciated for its individual voices as much as the whole.

These, and so many other of Bach's works, are endlessly rewarding for the right brain.

---

40 See 'The Role of the Artist in Society', Ettlinger, L.D. in *The Eighteenth Century*, Thames and Hudson, London 1969
41 See *Art Treasures of the World* Hamlyn Publishing Group, London 1970
42 *The Cambridge Music Guide* Cambridge University Press 1990, pp140-143
43 Idem.

44 McGilchrist points us to a study by Vollmer-Haase, Finke, Harje et al, 1998, showing that the contrapuntal music of Bach causes a strong right-hemisphere reaction. They suggest that the individual melodic lines need to be maintained in consciousness simultaneously and this requires the right brain to hold the experience in working memory.
45 *The Master and His Emissary,* p420

46 See *Bach*, from *The Master Musicians* series, Malcom Boyd, J.M. Dent & Sons, London 1983
47 *The Master and His Emissary,* p420
48 *Erbarme dich* has been described by Sir Yehudi Menuhin as "the most beautiful piece of music ever written for the violin" and "the centre and synthesis of western music" by Polish poet Adam Zagajewski. See 'My music is better because I work harder': Bach's *St. Matthew Passion*, Haven, C., 2013

24
Top
Grand Canal Looking Northeast from the Palazzo Balbi to the Rialto Bridge, Canaletto c.1719

Note the depiction of depth, the movement in the sky, how a moment in time is caught in the transitory passing of a cloud and the shadow it casts, the naturalistic depiction of light and shade, and the visual ambiguity that ensues, drawing the eye into the painting.

25
Right
Grand staircase of Der Residenz, Wurzburg, by architect Balthasar Neumann 1744

This was a period of artistic collaboration, when architects worked alongside painters. The Venetian painter Giovanni Battista Tiepolo and his son, Domenico, painted the frescoes in the building.

But the second half of the 18th century was very different. This was a period of replication and productivity, a period when it was felt that all questions could be answered.[49] In 1776, modern economics was established when Adam Smith published his *Wealth of Nations*, in which he observes how the organisation of workers into specialised roles leads to greater productivity.[50] Matthew Boulton and James Watt perfected the steam engine (1788) and Richard Arkwright mass produced cotton yarn in new manufactories using looms powered by water. Modern manufacturing and the replication of goods was born. Jeremy Bentham brought us *utilitarianism*, and his "projects were those of classification", inventing "the words *international, codify and maximise*" and writing that "the community is a fictitious body".[51] This was also a period of professionalisation in Europe's armies, navies and in diplomacy, ushering in war on a new scale.[52]

"The greatest improvement in the productive powers of labour and the greater part of the skill, dexterity, and judgement with which it is anywhere directed, or applied, seem to have been the effects of the division of labour."
Adam Smith

Thus, the sensuality of the Baroque period quickly gave way to a new sense of scientific moralism and appropriateness; we have veered back to left-brain attentional preferences. In painting, a rather self-conscious period saw the portrait come into vogue in the hands of Sir Joshua Reynolds and Sir Thomas Gainsborough, and even faces in portraiture were represented more symmetrically in this period.[53] Sir Joshua Reynolds wrote in 1770 in relation to a young artist's training, "The wish of the genuine painter must be more extensive: instead of endeavouring to amuse mankind with minute neatness of his imitations, he must endeavour to improve them by the grandeur of his ideas".[54] This echoes Koerner's description of the Reformation, when "ideas about the thing, not the thing itself" became important; a sentiment that could be said to describe the prevailing view in advertising today. Reynolds' *Discourses* also criticised Bernini and the Renaissance for portraying mixed emotions; the spirit of the time was rather one of "clarity and precision".[55] Tastes in music changed quickly and the work of Bach, Vivaldi and Telemann was soon considered old-fashioned and too complex, and they were forgotten.[56] Musicians in the Classical period "were eager to simplify and regularize the language of music and regarded the style of their immediate forebears as extravagant and irregular".[57] In the hands of Gluck and Haydn music became more measured, straightforward, restrained and, by and large, harmonically less interesting, less spontaneous. It merits note, that of Haydn's 104 symphonies, 93 are written in the major key.

"This was a time when virtually all composers pursued the same basic ideas as to how music should be constructed: the idea of balance between keys, to give the listener a clear sense of where the music was going, and between sections, so that the listener was always correctly oriented within a piece and had a good idea what to expect of it."[58]

If there were forms to be followed in music, then in architecture there were pattern books, showing how you might replicate classically inspired designs for churches, houses and other buildings. A desire for symmetry and order in architecture pervaded, and it is of note that the plan and styles of religious buildings in post-Reformation Protestant Europe were by and large more rectilinear than those in Catholic countries.[59]

The *Enlightenment's* focus on rationality led it to propose a moral and legal basis for the state. In France, Rousseau's *Contrat Social* (1762) asserted that every person was born with certain rights – the contract was fixed and uniform – and that it was the government's duty to uphold these on behalf of the general will. This necessarily resulted in the loss of individual liberty in exchange for a common "pooled sovereignty".[60] This gave revolutionaries new ideas about the role of government and, in an act of left-brain sophistry (the left brain rejects anything outside its model of the world), anyone who opposed their ideas was deemed a 'tyrant'. To counter inflation, the *Law of The Maximum* was introduced to control and standardise prices, contravention of which brought the death penalty, echoing Diocletian's Tetrarchy.

If the *Reformation* had seen a transfer of power from the Catholic Church to the state, the *French Revolution* was openly secular in its intent.[61] The decapitation of effigies in the *Reformation* had a gruesome counterpart in the *French Revolution*. As McGilchrist points out, the left brain, with its desire to look at the parts, to chop up the whole into its constituent parts, even the human body, found its apotheosis in the guillotine.[62] Jeaurat de Berty's *Allegory on the Revolution* gives us an insight into the left brain's influence at the time of *The Terror*.

26
**Allegory on the Revolution,
Jeaurat de Bertry 1794**

Note the abstracted scenes
presented by the painter, with no
coherent sense of a whole. Note
the abstracted spolia;
part-columns and fragments of
buildings with words depicting the
concepts of liberté and égalité.
Note the symbols of the
Revolution – the axes and red cap
and the tree of liberty – all
presided over by the Eye of Truth
and Rousseau. The Eye of Truth
bears a striking resemblance to
the single eyes in the drawings of
those suffering psychotic
episodes, a symptom associated
with schizophrenia and right-brain
hypofunction. 'The eyes of history
are upon us' is a phrase we hear a
great deal today.

49 McGilchrist refers us to Sir Isiah Berlin, who explains there are "three propositions [..] upon which the whole Western tradition rested": namely, "that all genuine questions can be answered, that if a question cannot be answered it is not a question"; "that all answers are knowable, that they can be discovered by means which can be learnt and taught to other persons" and "that the answers must be compatible with one another", *The Master and His Emissary*, p336
50 See 'The Economics of an Age of Change', Coleman, D.C. in *The Eighteenth Century*, Thames and Hudson, London 1969

51 *The Master and his Emissary*, p340. Bentham's utilitarianism would later inspire Dickens' *Hard Times* (1854)
52 See 'Professionalism in armies, navies and diplomacy', Western, J. R. in *The Eighteenth Century*, Thames and Hudson, London 1969
53 *The Master and His Emissary*, p343
54 See 'The Role of the Artist in Society', Ettlinger, L.D. in *The Eighteenth Century*, Thames and Hudson, London 1969
55 *The Master and His Emissary*, p337
56 Mozart and Beethoven, of course, continued to recognise Bach's significance

57 *The Cambridge Music Guide*, Cambridge University Press 1990, p140
58 Idem. p219
59 'Royalty, Religion and the Urban Background, The Architectural Setting', Summerson, J., Sir, in *The Eighteenth Century*, Thames and Hudson, London 1969
60 'Free Enquiry and the World of Ideas', Shackleton, R., in *The Eighteenth Century*, Thames and Hudson, London 1969
61 *The Master and His Emissary*, p347
62 *The Master and His Emissary*, p348

27
Above
Moon Rising Over the Sea,
Caspar David Friedrich 1821

28
Left
Giant Mountains
(View of the Small Sturmhaube
from Warmbrunn),
Caspar David Friedrich 1810

Listening note 4
Der Jüngling an der Quelle
(The Boy by the Spring), D.300, a Schubert song 1817
Words by Freiherr Johann Gaudenz von Salis-Seewis

From Romanticism to Modernism.

Even before the events of the *French Revolution*, a new movement, *Sturm und Drang* ('Storm and Stress'), was emerging in Germany, given creative force by Goethe.[63] The movement stressed the importance of emotion, nature, subjectivity and of free expression, and evolved out of the constraining rational urges of the *Enlightenment*. This was the seed of Romanticism, which was given further impetus by the terrifying ideologies of the *French Revolution* and encroaching industrialisation. Many of the characteristics of the right brain come to the fore in the Romantic period. In art and music we see a connection with place and nature, with folklore, and a harking back to a time before the *Enlightenment*. Depth and visual ambiguity (half-light, dawn, dusk) become very pronounced in art and there is a pre-occupation with dreams.[64] It was a period of individual difference and a sense that a thing and its opposite could both be true.[65] A new sense of flow and spontaneity was embraced in music. The space between people – even and especially in separation – is seen in music and in art; a new emphasis is placed on touch, melancholy and longing (remember while the left brain *wants*, the right brain *yearns*).

Leise, rieselnder Quell!	Softly burbling brook,
Ihr wallenden, flispernden Pappeln	swaying, whispering poplars,
Euer Schlummergeräusch	your slumberous murmur
Wecket die Liebe nur auf.	only stirs love in me.
Linderung sucht' ich bei euch,	Consolation in you I sought,
Und sie zu vergessen, die Spröde;	And to forget she who is so aloof.
Ach, und Blätter und Bach	But alas, the leaves and the brook
Seufzen, Luise, dir nach!	sigh, Louise, after you!

Schubert was the master of the *Lied* (song) in its numerous forms. He took inspiration from many different poets and chose his material with great care. He was also unafraid to change the words when he felt it would improve the overall effect (the right-brained 'whole'). The final couplet in the song above originally ran 'Elisa mir zu' ('the leaves and brook sigh to me Elisa'), but Schubert changed this to the version printed here, presumably because it scans better with 'Bach'; but this also changes the meaning so that our boy is now *yearning after Elisa* (Schubert also changed the name to Louise, which is more pleasant to sing).[66] The song ends with a plaintive, dying 'Louise' (not printed here but always sung). The piano accompaniment conveys a youthful and wistful sense of expectation. Contrast this with the approach Haydn took to his songs in the Classical period – he set music to texts chosen for him by others, which have been described as "monotonously strophic".[67]

The evocation of place, flow, longing and belonging would continue in music late into the 19th century, with composers such as Chopin, Smetana, Grieg, Dvorak, Albeniz and Granados rooting their work in the sounds of the folk tradition. Chopin's Mazurkas were influenced by the Polish *mazur* folk dance and his Nocturnes ('songs of the night') by John Field's compositions.[68]

It is noteworthy that Bach was rediscovered and celebrated in this period by Mendelssohn, and that Liszt should also look back to transcribe many of Bach's works for piano, as well as many of Schubert's songs. The Romantic period was a time when musicians and artists showed an interest in work that had gone before – just as in the Renaissance. In Wagner, there was a nostalgia for a heraldic past. An intense longing in eternal separation can too be heard in his *Liebestod*.[69]

The right brain's sense of depth, place, betweenness, awe before nature and its liking for visual ambiguity, is felt very keenly in Caspar David Friedrich's landscape paintings. We see depth and visual ambiguity in the penumbra and mists of his landscapes and seascapes. Note in *Moon Rising Over the Sea* (Illustration 27) the sense of betweenness – one woman touches and comforts another, they both look out upon the two men, who in turn look out on the boats. There is a sense of longing. Unlike the artworks of left-brain periods, the painting asks more questions than it seeks to answer. In *Giant Mountains* (Illustration 28), we also see depth and visual ambiguity in a technique known as *aerial perspective* – the mountains behind are painted ever more faintly in receding planes of depth. The painting captures a moment in time, as a cloud passes over the middle distance, the sun lighting up for a moment the slopes in the foreground. In *Wanderer above the Sea of Fog* (Illustration 29), note the height, the depth and the visual ambiguity conveyed by the artist. The central figure has his back to us and looks out in awe over nature, aware of his place in the world and his connection to it.

63 *The Oxford Companion to German Literature*, Garland, M., Oxford University Press, Oxford 1991
64 McGilchrist points to evidence showing that dreaming lateralises to the right, and are part of the re-integration process, *The Master and His Emissary*, p189 and p198
65 *The Master and His Emissary*, p353
66 Graham Johnson, Hyperion 1995
67 *The Penguin Book of Lieder*, Edited and translated by S.S. Prawer, Penguin, London 1964
68 *The Cambridge Music Guide*, Cambridge University Press 1990, pp315-320
69 Isolde looks upon her beloved Tristan after he has died and hallucinates that he is coming back to life. The 'fragrances' about her eventually engulf her in bliss as she falls down dead next to him. As McGilchrist explains, smell plays an important part in social bonding and "grounding our world in intuition and the body"

The Romantic period would not last, and the left brain's influence would soon become apparent again in the arts, with greater emphasis than ever before.

The first half of the 20th century was a period of mechanisation – in manufacturing, transport and in war. The dangerous categorisation of people – and removal of those categories – becomes apparent in communism and fascism, which both exhibit the excesses of the left brain – its demand for control, centralisation and absolute denial of alternative perspectives. An increasingly mechanised society was soon reflected in art that was decontextualised, flat and abstracted. Turner's Romanticism in the 19th century gave way to Impressionism and then to Pointillism, and ultimately to Cubism, Dadaism and Futurism in the Twentieth. As is the left-brain preference, Futurism emphasised man-made 'things' – technology, cities, cars, aeroplanes, buildings, streets – and a sense of menace or violence.[70] And as in art, in music; Schoenberg, Stockhausen and Cage brought music to the world that was atonal, dissonant, abstract and increasingly conceptual – as McGilchrist puts it, that is "hard to appreciate intuitively".[71] Schoenberg is indeed meant to have said, "How the music sounds is not the point".[72] John Cage's *4'33"* (1952) instructs the performer *not* to play their instrument for exactly four minutes and thirty-three seconds. Cage wanted audiences to listen to the sounds about and within themselves.[73] In true left-brained fashion, and as we have seen in other periods, the *concept had become the thing.* Cage's work was a shocking rejection of music, as much as contemporary Rauschenberg's white canvasses were a rejection of art (1951). The piece was controversial; it was what we might describe today, as 'disruptive'.

We will return to the notion of *disruption* in Section 5, but in the next section we'll examine today's cultural landscape, and changes in advertising styles in the recent past.

29
Wanderer above the Sea of Fog
Caspar David Friedrich 1818

"**Newness** (seeing afresh what one thought of as familiar, as though for the first time — the patient process of Romanticism) **and novelty** (deliberately disturbing the representation of reality in an attempt to 'shock oneself' into something that feels unfamiliar) **are contrary concepts.**"

Iain McGilchrist

70 See *Art Treasures of the World*, Hamlyn Publishing Group, London 1970
71 *The Master and His Emissary*, p 418
72 McGilchrist refers us to *Philosophy of Modern Music*, Adorno, T., Seabury Press, New York 1973
73 *The Cambridge Music Guide*, Cambridge University Press 1990

Section 2
Summary.

In both paintings opposite, there is a striking resemblance to the everyday objects drawn by the left brain in Nikolaenko's experiments (see Illustration 3). As McGilchrist explains, "Viewed from a psychological standpoint, modernist art appears to mimic the world as it would appear to someone whose right hemisphere was inactivated; in other words, it brings into being the world of the left hemisphere".[74]

30
Opposite top
Interior with a girl drawing,
Pablo Picasso 1935

Note the deliberate flatness, a distortion of perspective, the self-consciousness of the sitter painting herself in front of the mirror.

31
Opposite bottom
Le Port, Joan Miro 1945

Here flatness is taken still further; note the abstraction and, again, the single eyes.

1 The brain is divided and asymmetrical; the two hemispheres differ structurally and are joined only by the *corpus callosum*, which bridges the two brains but also allows one hemisphere to inhibit the other at any given time. The *corpus callosum* has been getting proportionally smaller and functionally more inhibitory over human history, and the left hemisphere has a greater suppressive effect on the right brain than the right on the left.

2 The two hemispheres have different takes on the world and attend to it differently. The left hemisphere favours narrow, short and focused attention; the right hemisphere brings broad and vigilant focus to bear on the world.

3 The right hemisphere experiences the world as it is, it sees the whole, understands the world through connections, relationships and embodied experience, sees depth and appreciates lived time, attends to novelty, deals with contradiction and therefore understands ambiguity, metaphor and humour. It is self-aware and has a sense of proportion and perspective.

4 The left hemisphere abstracts things from their context and represents the world through mental models. It is goal oriented, seeking to manipulate and control the world through tools, through language and categorisation. It sees linear cause and effect, is self-conscious, literal, explicit and dogmatic, cutting off anything outside its model of the world.

5 People, societies and companies need hemispheric balance to flourish, and through history we can observe periods of such hemispheric balance in creativity of the age – in art, literature, sculpture, architecture and music. But the left brain tends to overreach itself, and in other periods we see left-brain characteristics come to the fore.

6 Periods of whole-brained creativity are characterised by collaboration, community, a very broad and heightened sense of one's time and place in the world, a sense of responsibility for one's own actions, a fascination for difference, and a greater sense of empathy, all reflecting the right brain's way of attending to the world. Attention is broad and sustained. These periods are questioning and seek possibility – 'I wonder whether...?' There is a depth and humanity to culture, a referencing of other things, a sense of flow; the living and betweenness are prioritised.

7 Periods of left-brained creativity are characterised by a desire for power and control, by hierarchy, rules, repetition, centralisation, standardisation, categorisation and specialisation. Society becomes rigid and brittle, those with alternative views are closed down, things are interpreted literally, there is a sense of dislocation from place, other people and the past, a lack of empathy and an intolerance, a heightened sense of paranoia, anger and self-consciousness. Attention is narrow and brief. There is a loss of uniqueness. Instead there is a sense of repetition and homogeneity. These periods are didactic and focused on what is 'right' – 'I know that ... (and you should too)'. Culture becomes flatter, more abstract, conceptual and self-conscious, and words and symbols take on a new importance.

An increase in abstraction and
flatness, a reliance on rhythm,
and an emphasis on unilateral
messaging

Section 3
What's happening today:
An Historic Cultural Shift

Nations divided.

The last twenty-five years have brought enormous technological change. In less than a generation, communication has changed beyond recognition; the ability of almost anyone to reach people wherever they are and in ever greater numbers is unprecedented. If society and culture saw changes following the introduction of the Gutenberg printing press, then it would not be unreasonable to expect to see similar changes in culture and society following the digital revolution, and to see them happen more quickly than ever before. But before we bring our story up to date, let's step back to a period immediately before today, to a period that, for some, is still within living memory.

The 1960s brought a cultural and creative revolution in the West. It manifested itself not in high culture, which, as we saw in the last section, had become increasingly conceptual and abstract, but found an outlet in *popular* culture. In Britain, a new generation of children who had grown up with post-war rationing and good levels of education in both the sciences and the humanities were fast becoming adults. The 'teenager' was finding its voice, and the decade saw old formalities swept away. Among the young, there was a sense of aspiration and irreverence, a sense of possibility and social mobility. A period of collaboration and craft manifested itself in a new wave of film, music, comedy, fashion and, of course, commercial television. American Blues and Country influences arrived in the UK and intermingled with the British hymnal and music-hall tradition with memorable results.[75] Columbia Records made Robert Johnson's 1930s Mississippi Delta Blues guitar playing (itself the intersection between "black melody and rhythm and white harmony and meter"[76]) commercially available to the general public, and so Johnson posthumously influenced Muddy Waters, Bob Dylan, Jimi Hendrix, Keith Richards, Eric Clapton and Robert Plant. Folk and jazz influences, experimentation and amplification led to new and varied musical genres, which sung of protest, but also of the bittersweet experiences of love and youth. New pirate radio stations in the North Sea ensured that these sounds could be heard in ever greater numbers. A scan of the song titles of the folk – and indeed pop and rock – music of the 1960s and 1970s will reveal, in today's context, a strikingly right-brain take on the world, with all its fondness for betweenness, longing, place and the passing of time: James Taylor's *Long ago and Far Away* and *Places in My Past*, Carole King's *So Far Away*, *It's Going to Take Some Time*, Fairport Convention's *Who Knows Where the Time Goes*, The Rolling Stones' *Miss You* or *Memory Girl*. The wistful folk guitar music of Nick Drake, Bert Jansch and Wizz Jones also speak of a right-brain preference for ambiguity, longing and melancholy.

But the last twenty-five years have seen a marked cultural shift, where any voice temporarily given to the right brain in popular culture has been reclaimed by the left brain. The 21st century has ushered in a period of left-brain dominance that can be seen in television programming, film franchises, music and music lyrics. And as we shall also see, in advertising.

Few would contest that the West today is divided. People have taken on entrenched political positions, and define themselves in opposition to others, with worryingly little desire to understand others' points of view. There is anger and protest. Karl Marx's grave and other monuments to people and the past are being defaced and destroyed, art is being removed from institutions and galleries. We are caught up in our mobile phones; selfies and mirror selfies have become normal. Society is increasingly self-conscious and obsessed with body image. Pubs – places of community – are closing[77] and gym membership is increasing;[78] people are prioritising solitary gym repetitions in front of a mirror over going to the pub with their friends. Bars that provide a focused activity for their clientele, a competitive game such as mini golf or table tennis, are increasingly prevalent. New rules have emerged on how we behave towards each other. Universities – places of learning and debate – now 'no platform' those with controversial views. We're a society increasingly under surveillance and people don't know which news media to trust; there is a sense of paranoia in the air. There's a fear of repeating the mistakes of the past but also of inadvertently causing offence. The public 'calling out' of behaviours on social media has become commonplace; there have been a succession of public 'shamings', verbal attacks and defences that are tribal in nature, and that suggest we have moved from a guilt to a shaming culture. Society is brittle and dislocated.

One might ask whether these are conditions conducive to creativity. These, and many others, are tell-tale signs that we have moved from a whole-brained to a left-brained society. As we saw in the last section, these changes in society around us will leave inevitable and visible traces in culture.

75 *The Cambridge Music Guide,* Cambridge University Press 1990, p510
76 Idem, p510
77 See https://www.economist.com/graphic-detail/2017/07/10/why-it-is-closing-time-for-so-many-london-pubs
78 See https://masterinvestor.co.uk/equities/pump-up-your-portfolio-with-the-gym-group/
79 *Measuring the Evolution of Contemporary Western Popular Music,* Serrà, J., Corral, A., Boguñá, M., Haro, M. and Arcos, J.L., *Scientific Reports* volume 2 Article number: 521 (2012)
80 *Are Pop Lyrics Getting More Repetitive?* Morris, C., The Pudding, https://pudding.cool/2017/05/song-repetition/

The effect on culture.

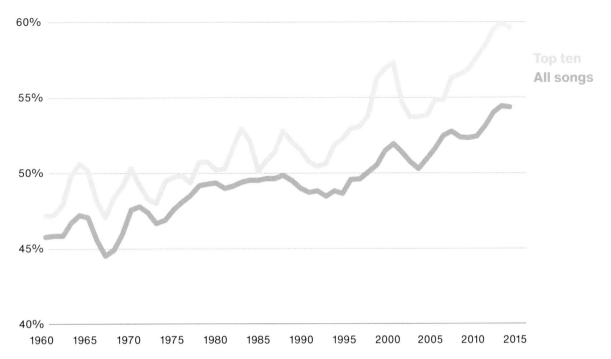

Fig 19 Repetition of lyrics within songs in pop music by year Analysis Colin Morris

The observation that music isn't what it used to be is generally an indication that we're getting older, but there's evidence to suggest it might actually be true. A recent large-scale analysis of popular music (rock, pop, hip hop, metal and electronic) set out to examine the changes in pitch (harmonic content, encompassing chords, texture or tone), timbre (sound, texture or tone quality associated with instrument types, performance and recording techniques) and intrinsic recording loudness from 464,411 music recordings dating from 1955 to 2010. It concludes that music has become less varied in pitch progression, the timbral palette has homogenised (frequent timbres have become more frequent) and the average recording loudness has increased (which threatens dynamic richness).[79] Harmony is the aural equivalent of depth, so music has, in a sense, 'flattened' in this period.

There has also been a narrowing in the range of music lyrics. Colin Morris uses compression software on song lyrics to establish their repetitiveness within a given song, using a dataset of 15,000 songs that charted on the Billboard Hot 100 between 1958 and 2017. His analysis suggests that since the turn of the 21st century, there has been a sharp increase in the repetitiveness of song lyrics, in particular those reaching the top 10 in the charts.[80]

Repetition and a desire for predictability is also evident in the types of films that are being made. An analysis of the top 10 grossing films every year going back to 1980 reveals a startling trend towards the franchise, which first became apparent in 2002. From 1980-2001, the average number of franchise films in the top 10 grossing UK films was 2.2. Since 2002, the average number of franchise films in the top 10 grossing films has been 5.7. It was the first decade of the 21st century that this shift first became manifest.

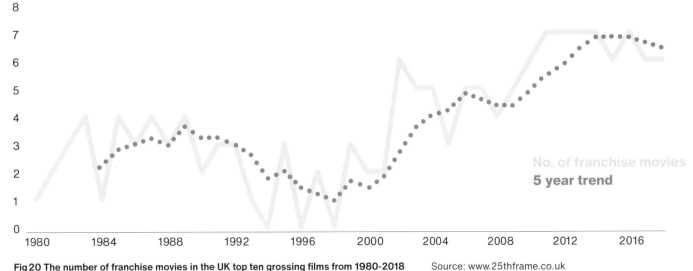

Fig 20 The number of franchise movies in the UK top ten grossing films from 1980-2018   Source: www.25thframe.co.uk

Left brain

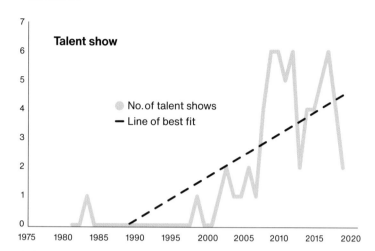

Fig 21 **The rise of the talent show: the proportion of the top 10 viewed shows each year that were talent shows from 1980-2018. Note both recorded and live shows are represented** source: BARB

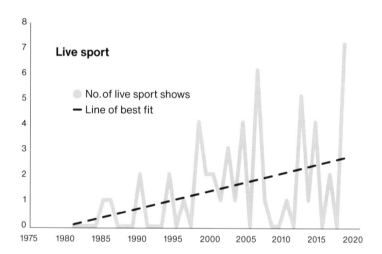

Fig 22 **The rise of live sport: the proportion of the top 10 viewed shows each year that were live sport shows from 1980-2018** source: BARB

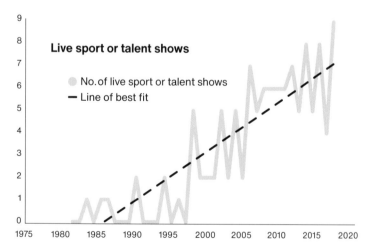

Fig 23 **The rise of the left brain in programming from 1980-2018: the proportion of the top 10 viewed shows each year is now dominated by either live sport or talent shows** source: BARB

Right brain

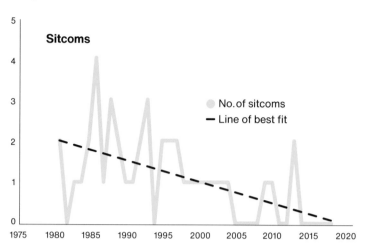

Fig 24 **The decline in the sitcom: the proportion of the top 10 viewed shows each year that were sitcoms from 1980-2018** source: BARB

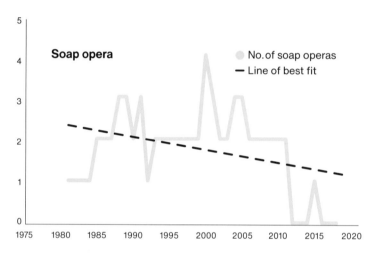

Fig 25 **The decline in the soap opera: the proportion of the top 10 viewed shows each year that were soap operas from 1980-2018** source: BARB

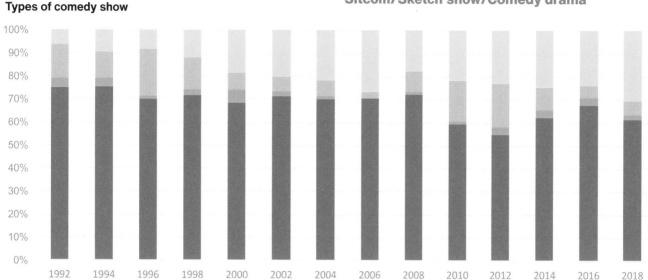

Types of comedy show

Documentary/Factual/Chat show/Panel show
Stand-up
Variety
Sitcom/Sketch show/Comedy drama

Fig 26 The loss of betweenness in comedy programmes and the rise of the factual (all BBC, ITV and C4 comedy shows aired 1992-2018) Source: www.comedy.co.uk

Television programming and viewing habits have also seen striking changes. The *number* of channels and programmes available in the UK has, of course, increased dramatically since 1980, but the *types* of programme that we watch have changed too. Looking at the BARB viewing figures back to 1980, we can see how programmes which celebrated betweenness, comedy or relationships – sitcoms and soap operas – no longer appear in the top 10 rated shows, while at the same time, shows that focus on competition, with rules, winners and repetitive formats – live sport and talent shows – dominate the most viewed programmes.

The right brain is responsible for understanding humour, so let's look more closely at the type of comedy programmes that have been made on UK television in this period.

The number of comedy programmes made on mainstream channels in the UK in this period has increased by 44%, so at first glance it seems that comedy programming is flourishing, in *output* terms at least. But the type of show that is being made and aired today is quite different from the type of show made and aired in the early 1990s.

The proportion of comedy shows relying on characters, relationships and betweenness (sitcoms, sketch shows and comedy drama) has fallen in this period by 19%. At the same time, there has been a dramatic increase in the

proportion of shows today *about comedy* (factual/ documentaries), that feature people talking *about other shows* (chat shows) or that are *factual* in nature (panel shows such as *QI, For Facts Sak*e) – a fivefold increase when taken together. This is noteworthy because these are either programmes about programmes (ideas about the thing, not the thing itself) or have an emphasis on factually improving us in some way.

Popular culture is, then, more repetitive, analytical, factual, competitive than it was a generation ago, and there is a new focus on *how things are made*. At the same time, there has been a loss in character, community and betweenness. The left brain's instincts for replicability, predictability, competition and the facts have reached into music, film and TV programming, at a time when the accessibility – and the amount – of content has never been greater. Popular culture has become manufactured.

Brands are not impervious to this shift. Just a glance at the changing styles of company logos in this period (Facebook, Microsoft, Apple – and recently BT) could be said to betray the left brain's instincts to flatten things. These are visible signs that marketers and designers are part of this cultural shift. There are also signs that the left brain has crept into advertising.

Flatland: exploring this cultural shift in advertising.

We might therefore hypothesise that advertising styles have also changed in the last twenty years and that left-brain features have become more prevalent. A visit to the Museum of Brands in London will leave you in no doubt that advertising reflects the culture of its time. It reflects it, but it also helps to create it.

A shift in advertising style towards one that embraces left-brain features would be a cause for concern. The right brain looks out for things of interest, for what stands out; it is attuned to novelty and ambiguity. The right brain is responsible for broad and vigilant attention, alert to the environment around us. It passes anything of interest to the left brain, which is responsible for focused attention, to unpack it, and give it back to the right brain in a process of synthesis and re-integration. If advertising is to get noticed, it needs in nearly every context to be of interest to the *right brain*. With the exception perhaps of paid search, we need to be creating work for the right brain, and indeed making the most of the right brain to create it.

The first step in identifying any changes in creative style is to define the features we're looking for. What would left-brain TV or video advertising look and sound like?

We'd expect it to be more goal oriented, literal, focused on things (the product) rather than people, to deliver a message and present the 'facts'. It would look flat, have no depth or perspective, no backdrop. It would favour abstraction, show the parts or features of things (e.g. the car mirror) or body (e.g. the mouth) rather than the whole. People would be devitalised, expressionless, presented as statues. Because the left brain's primary tool is language, it would feature unilateral communication – prominent voiceover, monologue to camera or regular metered prose. Words would obtrude upon the visuals, spelling out what you should be thinking and how you should be reacting to what you're seeing. Because it lacks an appreciation of lived time, it would favour fast-paced snapshot montages or freeze-frame effects over free-flowing drama. Soundtracks would become increasingly rhythmic. It would lose all cultural references, become self-referential and self-conscious.

It would shun things that only the right brain understands, first and foremost the living – so no room for characters, betweenness, dialogue or drama. It would have no sense of context, so no discernible sense of place, but would also be blind to history, so no historical settings, costumes or scene setting. Accents and other embodied vocal mannerisms would disappear. It would restrict ambiguity, double meaning, wordplay, knowing glances, implicit connection. It would proscribe flirtation, romance and humour. It would strip back music, shun melody, harmony, full timbre or anything in the minor key; in a bid to compensate for what it had lost, it would instead feel loud and energetic. Advertising would shun metaphor – or feel the need to explain it – and undervalue awe. It would lose its self-awareness.

Left-brain advertising would look flat, have no depth or perspective, no backdrop. It would spell out what you should be thinking and how you should be reacting ...

Left-brain features

1 Flatness
2 Abstracted product, feature, ingredient
3 Abstracted body part (e.g. hands, eyes, mouth, face)
4 Words obtrude during the ad
5 Voiceover
6 Monologue (e.g. testimonial)
7 Adjectives used as nouns (e.g. experience 'amazing')
8 Freeze-frame effect
9 Audio repetition (metered prose, sound effects)
10 Highly rhythmic soundtrack

Right-brain features

1 A clear sense of place
2 One scene unfolding with progression
3 Characters with agency (voice, movement, flow, expression)
4 Implicit, unspoken communication (e.g. knowing glances)
5 Dialogue
6 Distinctive accents
7 Play on words or subversion of language
8 Set in the past (costumes and sets)
9 Reference to other cultural works (pastiche/parody)
10 Music with discernible melody

Fig 27 Summary of left- and right-brain features that might be found in advertising

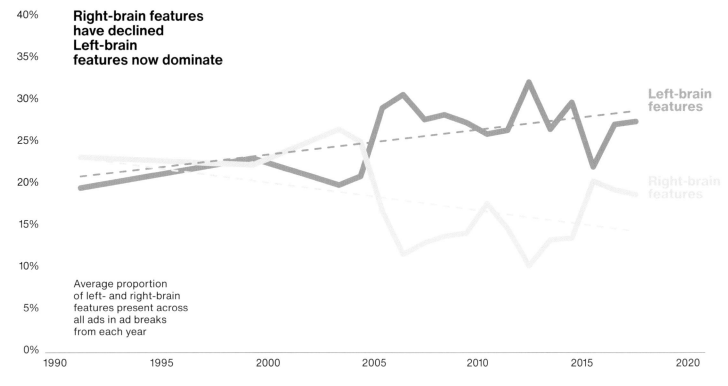

**Right-brain features
have declined
Left-brain
features now dominate**

Left-brain
features

Right-brain
features

Average proportion
of left- and right-brain
features present across
all ads in ad breaks
from each year

40%
35%
30%
25%
20%
15%
10%
5%
0%

1990   1995   2000   2005   2010   2015   2020

**Fig 28 Analysis of 620 ads appearing in *Coronation Street* ad breaks from week 40
2004-2018;** 29 ads from 1989, 1990, 1995 breaks (shown as 1992) and 38 ads
from 1996, 1997, 1999 and 2003 breaks (shown as 2000)

An historical analysis of advertising over the last thirty years allows us to investigate any changes in advertising style. *Coronation Street* is a long-running UK TV show that has remained on the same channel for sixty years, with consistently high audience figures and advertising value. It is possible to reconstruct the ad breaks from any given week for every year going back to 2004 with Nielsen data. We identified week 40 as a typical and unremarkable week – no holidays, no seasonal sales, no clock changes. Nielsen does not hold comprehensive advertising data prior to 2004, but given the changes outlined elsewhere, this is exactly the period we are interested in investigating, so we have supplemented this data with complete *Coronation Street* ad breaks recorded by enthusiasts and uploaded on YouTube from a number of different years in the years before.

We do not have data for every year for the years prior to 2004 and nor do we have as much data for those years, so we have aggregated the data and presented it as 1992 and 2000 to supplement the Nielsen data. The coding was conducted blind; the year of the advertising was masked and so unknown to the coder.

The analysis reveals that a marked change in advertising style has occurred in the first decade of the 21st century. Hemispheric balance has been lost. Left-brain features now dominate, where right-brain features once had the marginal upper hand.

Let's look at which features are being lost and what is replacing them.

The loss of right-brain features.

The first notable casualty is an implicit sense of betweenness. Conveying connection between people through gestures, facial expression or knowing glances is much less commonplace than it used to be. Characters' physical and verbal idiosyncrasies are important for memorability, but the inherent quiddity or 'whatness' of those depicted on screen has also been affected – accents, for instance, are much less common than they were. The right brain has a capacity to play with language and subvert it, but wordplay is also marginally less apparent than it used to be. Advertising is also less likely to depict a scene unfolding – a dramatic scene acted out before the audience. Music with a discernible melody is also much less prevalent than it was. But perhaps most worrying of all – because it shows how self-referential and self-conscious modern-day advertising is – is the decline in the number of ads referencing other cultural works, which includes pastiche or parody.

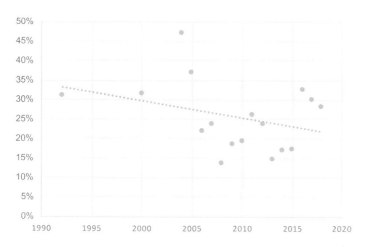

Fig 29 The loss of implicit communication
(character connection/betweenness, e.g. flirtation, knowing glances)

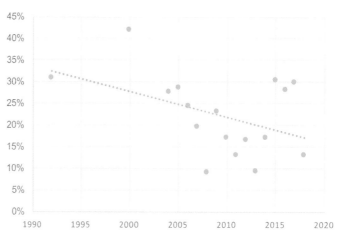

Fig 32 The loss of scenes unfolding (e.g. beginning middle and end)

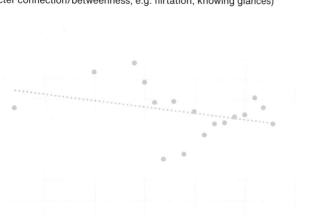

Fig 30 The loss of distinctive accents

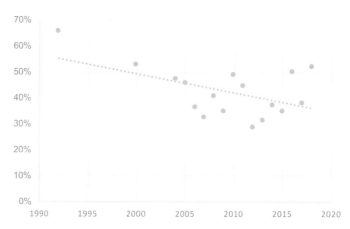

Fig 33 The loss of music with discernible melody

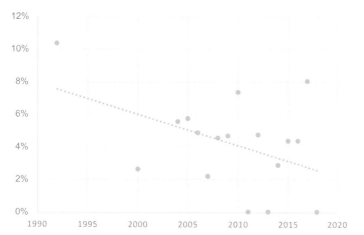

Fig 31 The loss of wordplay or subversion of language

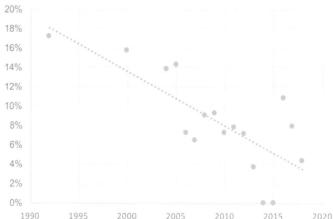

Fig 34 The loss of cultural references (pastiche/parody)

The rise of left-brain features.

Conversely, we see an increase in rhythmic soundtracks. We also see an increase in unilateral communication – monologues or voiceover where the viewer is addressed directly. The obtrusion of words on the screen is also a noteworthy development, much as it was in the artwork of the *Reformation*. The left brain also seeks to turn descriptive adjectives into nouns (it's much more comfortable with things), and so we increasingly see expressions such as

'small just works' in advertising today. Flatness – a lack of depth, perspective or background – has also become increasingly commonplace, betraying a lack of empathy.

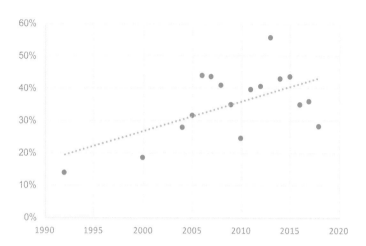

Fig 35 The rise of the rhythmic soundtrack

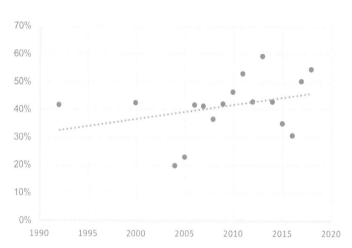

Fig 38 The rise of the word obtruding on the ad (before end frame)

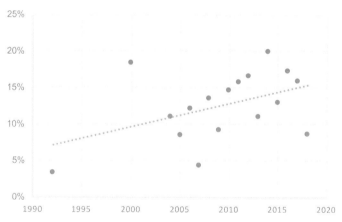

Fig 36 The rise of the monologue (unilateral communication)

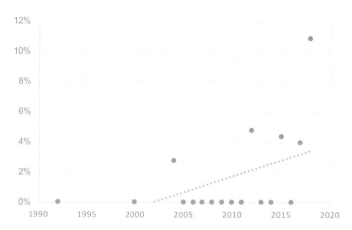

Fig 39 The rise of adjectives used as nouns

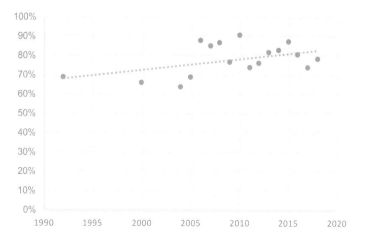

Fig 37 The rise of the voiceover (unilateral communication)

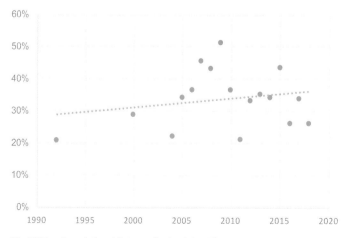

Fig 40 The rise of visual flatness (lack of depth)

Illustrating the shift.

Let's examine two ads made over thirty years apart, which exemplify the dramatic shift in style – Lowe-Howard-Spink's 1985 *Water In Majorca* ad for Heineken and GoDaddy's 2018 *Make Your Own Way* ad.

The Heineken ad is written, directed and performed to get the right brain's attention. At the risk of explaining the joke, let's look at it frame by frame.

First, it has a clear sense of place and context. From the first moment of the ad, we know where we are – the 'School of Street Credibility' – and that this is most likely a conceit. There is a dog barking off screen, the shadow of a person moving in the next room and there's traffic noise outside. This sense of realism is extremely important, because it makes the subversion of reality in all that follows all the more entertaining.

Del arrives. The right brain susses him out – he's younger than the teacher and from the teacher's manner we assume Del must be an assistant. We can tell from Del's manner that he's bored and has to put up with a lot from the teacher.

As soon as we see them, we know they have been there a long time: the woman is rather upright and stiff; the man is fed up and stares out the window in dismay. Their accents tell us that they are from different social backgrounds and the room that this is a lesson. Something's wrong with the grammar in the rhyme on the board. The student reads it out in a plummy accent, changing 'don't' to the more correct 'doesn't'.

Del hands her a beer (so that we can see the label). 'Ere y'are. Get ya laughin' gear round that.' Again, the right brain plays with language. The student looks as though she's never seen anything of the like before.

The camera swings round to get in the space between the characters, giving us a slightly different perspective. The teacher gets up, frustration on his face, placing his hands carefully on the desk for extra emphasis, 'No, no, no...' and sounds it out, leaning forward over the desk. The student mouths along with him, as if trying to learn a foreign language.

Reaction shot back to teacher, shaking his head, still despairing.

Trying to please, the student has another go, indefatigable hope and innocence in her voice and face. She changes the grammar again, to make it read more elegantly, 'The water in Majorca doesn't taste quite how it should?' Her accent and dress, together with a subtle and re-strained flick of the wrist – seeing off the phrase with delicate emphasis – implicitly signal that she's upper class.

She opens the can. From her hesitant body language, closed eyes and raised eyebrows the right brain senses she's slightly uncomfortable with the idea of opening a can, has probably never done so before and that she struggles with the physical exertion of it.

We move from a close-up on the student's insouciant face to a headshot of the teacher.

She tries it. Eyes open wide and eyebrows raised.

A look of deep frustration on his brow: 'Oi, Del, any danger of some refreshment in 'ere?'

Note the irony and subversion of language, just the way the right brain likes it.

She speaks. Her accent changes and her whole face with it. Note the wider and looser mouth.

Water In Majorca ad for Heineken 1985

Reaction shot – 'What's that?'

The teacher's delighted, gets up, 'She's cracked it, she's only cracked it', allowing himself the luxury of loosening his tie in a moment of self-congratulation, and he puts his arm around Del.

There's a look of 'no real surprise' on Del's face, conveying a feeling that, yes, this is what happens from time to time. It could be described as the 'Stan Laurel' look.

But wait – something's happened to Del too. Meanwhile he's taken a swig and he's gone the other way and now sounds rather posh, 'Yah, epsolutely, Ron'. The teacher looks at Del as if he's lost his mind.

The student tries her newly found powers of elocution once more, this time louder, more confident, more pronounced. By now her whole face, body and manner have transformed.

In a moment, utter delight has passed from the teacher's face. He removes his hand from Del's shoulder and looks down at him despairingly. Del has another swig, unflustered, nonchalant, seemingly comfortable with the transformation. Maybe the achievement has more to do with the beer than the teacher.

She rounds off her rendition with a flourish – a triumphant sniff.

We end with the campaign's highly accented end line. But wait, even this has gone 'street cred' – 'Refreshes the parts wot other beers cannot reach'.

The ad is one single scene, performed by actors, and unfolds dramatically before us. The multiple reaction shots convey a strong sense of betweenness, and each actor brings something of themselves to the performance through their gestures, glances and mannerisms. The copywriting is succinct and not a word is wasted. There's a very right-brained subversion of language, a whatness and idiosyncrasy about the characters. An expressive face is centre screen most of the time, as is the can. The sparse dialogue is enormously important, but it is the performance and direction (Paul Weiland) of the ad – the knowing glances, facial expressions and body language that make it work. As well as referencing the famous scene in *My Fair Lady*, itself referencing *Pygmalion*, itself referencing Greek mythology, the whole ad is a metaphor for transformation (we will talk more about metaphor in section 5).

Adrian Holmes, the copywriter, had seen *My Fair Lady* one weekend and thought there was something of an idea in the 'Rain in Spain' scene. His colleague, Alan Waldie, pointed out it would be great for Heineken. They submitted a script, but they found they couldn't use the words because George Bernard Shaw was teetotal, and his estate wouldn't approve it. But the creative restraint led to a much better idea that played on a British prejudice of drinking the water in foreign countries. Majorca was a popular Spanish package holiday destination at the time and sounded good next to 'water'. The female lead is a caricature of the 'Sloane Ranger', an idea popularised by Peter York.

The piece sets up expectations and delays their fulfilment, rewarding us with surprise after surprise. It's funny and it's self-aware, and very pleasing for the right brain.[81]

81 Listen to *Stuff from the Loft,* Dave Dye, An interview with Adrian Holmes, for details of the ad's creative development

Make Your Own Way ad for GoDaddy 2018

It opens with an abstracted powder explosion and a devitalised face. Note the lack of depth or perspective. There is no sense of place. It's not clear where we are.

We switch quickly to a completely different scene. The word 'MAKE' in upper case obtrudes. There is unilateral communication – someone or something is telling us to do something.

We switch scene again. MAKE is now written differently. There's a person in a contorted and unnatural position on a podium.

We switch scene again. 'Your move' is written behind a woman exercising.

We switch scene again. A different woman is running on the spot.

We switch scene again. Now a man is skipping – performing repetitions in front of a set of mirrors. His image is replicated. There's a feeling of self-consciousness.

We switch scene again. There's a shadow of a boxing ring and a shadowy image of a boxer. A sense of menace and violence.

'Anthony's Gym' flashes up with a buy button, showing us how the left brain's sense of wanting can be fulfilled.

We move to a ghosted image of a woman. There's a sense of dislocation. The scene is flat.

We switch position to see her from above. The screen moves across as if she – and other women just like her – are on a conveyer belt. The word MAKE is repeated between each woman, dividing them up. The scene is flat.

We switch scene. An abstracted pair of earrings is subsumed in abstracted powder explosions; the words 'an impact' appear.

Another scene. More abstracted things to do with body image – this time make-up, with liquid make-up flowing backwards time-reversed out of the image.

"Its surfaces support words while its depths are filled with only what the words refer to." Joseph Leo Koerner (on Reformation Art)

Another scene.
Words on a flat background.

Another scene. A vase of flowers is abstracted into many pieces and 'MAKE' is once again superimposed.

Another scene, a devitalised face with dislocated letters flashed on to it.

Another scene – a flower display, 'your idea'.

Another scene. A laptop and a mobile, displaying the words, 'Get that uptown look'.

Abstracted liquid in water, images of make-up again, flower heads, 'a reality'.

Another object – a hairdryer set against a backdrop of horizontal lines. The left brain likes horizontal lines.

Man points finger at the audience – unilateral communication – and we are told, 'Make your own way'.

The hairdryer moves to the left, making way for a head, with face masked by hair, which appears from the right – the preferred field of view for the left brain.

GoDaddy

Another object – an E-type Jaguar.

The ad has many of the hallmarks of the left brain. It lacks perspective, and abstracts things and people from their context. The people featured bear no relation to each other. They only appear briefly; the primary focus is on *things*. Words obtrude. Communication is unilateral – the ad tells the audience to do something. There is little sense of flow – the scenes could almost be presented in any order; the only thing that links them is the words. As with Futurist art, there's a sense of dislocation and menace, and focus on cars and technology. The people are devitalised and move unnaturally. They are highly self-conscious (body image is clearly important), performing repetitive tasks like robots. The soundtrack is rhythmic and increasingly frenetic. The ad is focused on *making things* and using a *tool of the trade*.

The implications of Flatland for effectiveness.

If this were art, then perhaps these changes wouldn't matter so much. The change in style might not be to everyone's taste and, after all, who is to say what's right or wrong in matters of taste. Except that advertising isn't only an artform, it has a *commercial* purpose, and the effect of these changes is extremely damaging for advertising's ability to deliver long-term market-share growth.

In a separate analysis of recent advertising, System1 selected 100 UK and 100 US ads at random from System1's 2018 Ad Ratings database to determine the relationship between the presence of these left- and right-brain features and advertising effectiveness, as determined by System1's emotional Star rating score. The coding exercise was again

conducted blind – without the knowledge of the coder of the Star rating for the ads. The results are clear and significant – the greater the number of left-brain features in the ad, the less likely it is to achieve a strong Star rating; the greater the number of right-brain features in the ad, the more likely it is to achieve a high Star rating (the Star is rating a predictor of market-share growth potential, as outlined in section 1). Left-brain features are harmful to long-term growth and right-brain features are helpful.

Ads with more right-brain features have a clear advantage on the effectiveness Star rating over ads with fewer right-brain features (see Fig 42).

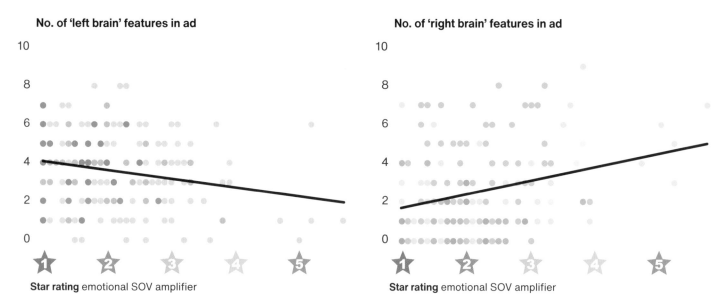

Fig 41 An analysis of 100 UK and 100 US TV ads selected at random from Automotive, Financial, FMCG, Health & Beauty and Tech sectors, showing the relationship between the presence of left- and right-brain features and Star rating

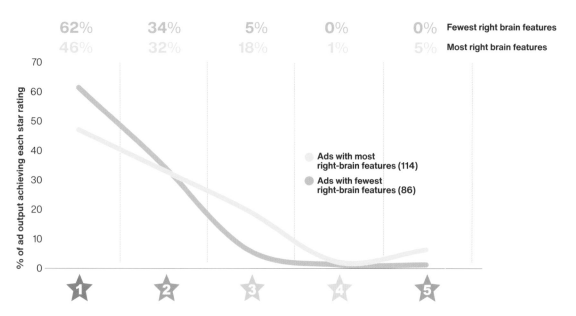

Fig 42 An analysis of 100 UK and 100 US TV ads selected at random from Automotive, Financial, FMCG, Health & Beauty and Tech sectors, showing the greater likelihood of ads with right-brain features to achieve stronger Star ratings

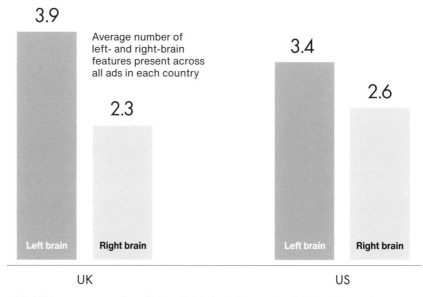

3.9

Average number of
left- and right-brain
features present across
all ads in each country

3.4

2.6

2.3

Left brain   **Right brain**   **Left brain**   **Right brain**

UK   US

Fig 43 The average number of left- and right-brain features in ads in the UK and US,
from a random sample of 100 UK and 100 US TV ads selected at random from Automotive,
Financial, FMCG, Health & Beauty and Tech sectors

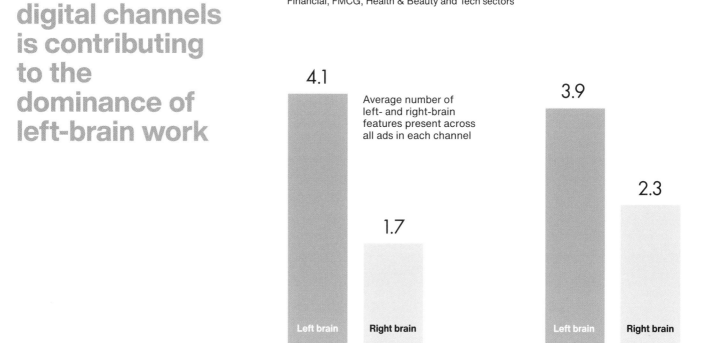

4.1

Average number of
left- and right-brain
features present across
all ads in each channel

3.9

2.3

1.7

Left brain   **Right brain**   **Left brain**   **Right brain**

UK YouTube   UK TV

**Fig 44 The average number of left- and right-brain features from a sample of 100 ads on
YouTube compared with a sample of 100 UK TV ads,** selected at random from Automotive,
Financial, FMCG, Health & Beauty and Tech sectors. YouTube ads include pre-, mid- and
post-rolls and range from 6 to 205 seconds

The use of digital channels is contributing to the dominance of left-brain work

This dataset also confirms the historical *Coronation Street* analysis, in that it shows that left-brain features are more prevalent than right-brain features on a randomly selected set of ads in two markets. If anything, it is more marked, and also reveals that the UK is further down the path to left-brain advertising than the US (see Fig 43).

An analysis of 100 randomly selected UK YouTube ads reveals an even more marked picture than the contemporary UK TV analysis. Left-brain features are even more dominant in ads appearing on YouTube than in ads on TV. The use of digital channels is contributing to the dominance of left-brain work, something we will return to in section 4.

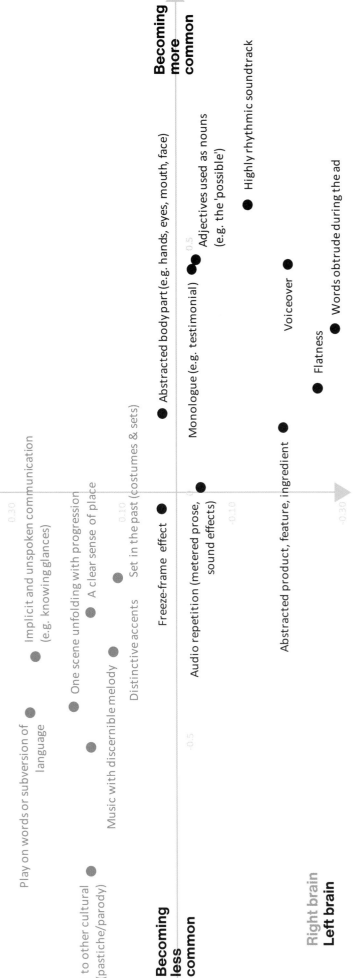

More effective

Becoming more common

Characters with agency (voice, movement, flow, expression)

Dialogue

Implicit and unspoken communication (e.g. knowing glances)

One scene unfolding with progression

A clear sense of place

Set in the past (costumes & sets)

Distinctive accents

Play on words or subversion of language

Music with discernible melody

Reference to other cultural works (pastiche/parody)

Abstracted body part (e.g. hands, eyes, mouth, face)

Adjectives used as nouns (e.g. the 'possible')

Highly rhythmic soundtrack

Monologue (e.g. testimonial)

Voiceover

Words obtrude during the ad

Flatness

Freeze-frame effect

Audio repetition (metered prose, sound effects)

Abstracted product, feature, ingredient

0.30

0.10

-0.10

-0.30

-0.5

0.5

Less effective

Becoming less common

Right brain
Left brain

Returning to the advertising data shown in Figs 41 and 43, it's clear that the features that are becoming more common are those that undermine long-term growth and the features that are disappearing from advertising are those that contribute most.

This is shown in detail in Fig 45.

Fig 45 Correlations between presence of features and effectiveness
(Star ratings, on the vertical axis) and between prevalence of features and year (less/more common, on the horizontal axis)

Mapping the change against the fall in effectiveness.

This harmful change in advertising style can be expressed as an index – the relationship between the number of left- and right-brain features in advertising over time, which we might call the *McGilchrist Index*. This index shows clearly that the balance between right- and left-brain features was lost in 2006.

Can this pronounced swing towards left-brain advertising be explained by a change in the composition of TV advertisers, perhaps? The swing towards left-brain advertising in 2006 certainly coincides with an increase in the number of retail ads in our sample (retail advertising in this period typically features many left-brain characteristics). But the answer is no. The same shift exists when we exclude retail ads and, moreover, when we look *within* sector over the measurement period, we see a **marked swing from right-brain to left-brain advertising styles in food, household goods, media and publishing, telecoms** and **fashion.** Many of these sectors are using TV less by the end of the measurement period, which points to two things:

1 that brands in these sectors are those that are switching to other (online) channels and **2** that the slight recovery we see for the right brain at the end of the measurement period is down to these increasingly left-brain categories using TV less.

This shift happened before the global downturn and the time period covered coincides with that reviewed in the 2019 IPA report *Crisis in Creative Effectiveness*. It was in 2008 that six-year rolling advertising effectiveness increases begin to slow before falling sharply in 2010; campaigns submitted in 2008 to the IPA Awards would have aired in the two years prior – from 2006. This fall in campaign effectiveness has been hitherto explained by an increase in short-termism and the re-allocation of budgets towards activation. But we now have another explanation for the fall in effectiveness: advertising style. **And the same attentional preference that lies behind short-termism, segmentation and tight targeting lies behind this shift in creative style.**

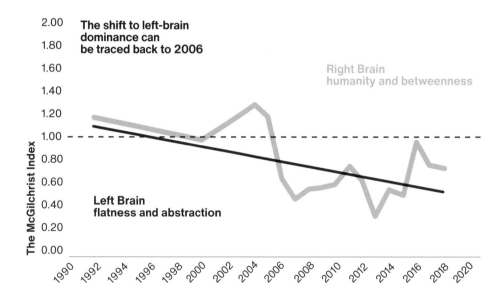

Fig 46 The *McGilchrist Index* reveals the loss of right-brain features in advertising in favour of left-brain features

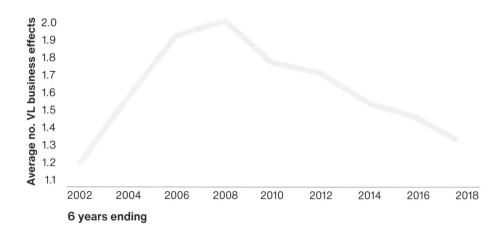

Fig 47 Advertising effectiveness is falling
From *The Crisis in Creative Effectiveness*, IPA, 2019

Effect on advertising's reputation.

It would be surprising if these changes in advertising style didn't harm the reputation of the advertising industry, and it's certainly true to say that the general public has a much less favourable view of it today than it used to. Data from Credos and the Advertising Association shows how favourability (often interpreted as 'trust') has declined markedly this century and how it has, in the period in question, all but collapsed.

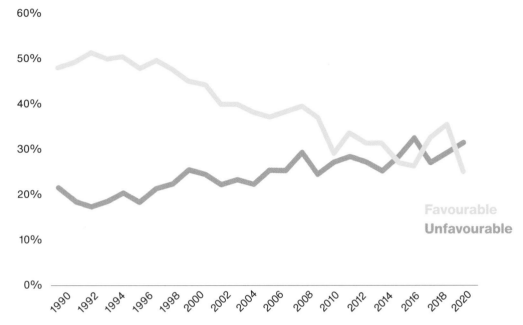

Favourable
Unfavourable

Fig 48 Favourability towards advertising Source: Credos

Martin Boase has been reported as once saying:

"We believe that if you're going to invite yourself into someone's living room for thirty seconds, you have a duty not to bore them or insult them by shouting at them. On the other hand, if you can make them smile, or show them something interesting or enjoyable – if you're a charming guest – then they may like you a bit better, and they may be a little more likely to buy your product".[82]

There was once an informal social contract between advertisers and the general public, where advertising understood that the public allowed advertisers into their homes on the understanding that advertisers entertained them. As Jonathan Haidt puts it, gratitude towards someone makes it easier to adopt their perspective.[83] As the ability of advertising to entertain has decreased, so has public trust.

If the quality of the work is declining, if the reputation of the industry is declining, it makes the advertising industry a much less attractive destination for creative school leavers or graduates.

So from every perspective, this is a problem that needs to be fixed. But to fix it, we first need to understand what might be causing it and how to guard against it; the subject of our next section.

" **The buying of time or space is not the taking out of a hunting license on someone else's private preserve but is the renting of a stage on which we may perform."**

Howard Gossage

Section 3 Summary.

1 An historic cultural shift has occurred in the West over the last three decades. The technological advances are evident, but so too are changes in society and culture.

2 In this period, we have witnessed marked changes in music, film, TV and comedy output and, significantly for us, in advertising.

3 The changes are consistent with a left-brain take on the world – a greater focus on productivity, standardisation, repetition, competition and the avoidance of risk. There's evidence that we're becoming more self-conscious and more analytical, that 'ideas about the thing' have become more important than 'the thing itself'.

4 Advertising styles have changed in this period, so that the features that contribute most to effectiveness are disappearing, and the features that work against effectiveness are now more commonplace.

5 These changes can be characterised as an increase in abstraction and flatness, a reliance on rhythm, and an emphasis on unilateral messaging, including the written word on-screen – features that appeal to the left brain. In the same period, advertising has been devitalised and dehumanised; we've lost dialogue, drama, implicit and knowing glances, gestures and accents. Advertising has become literal and self-conscious. It has lost its sense of betweenness, a right-brained appreciation of the living and lived experience. We've also lost a clear sense of time and place, music, wordplay and references to other cultural works.

6 The shift is not down to the changing composition of the advertising sectors using TV because it can be observed within sector.

7 These changes have occurred since 2006 and coincide with the loss of creative effectiveness reported separately by the IPA.

8 The same attentional preference that lies behind short-termism, segmentation and tight targeting lies behind this shift in creative style.

9 The shift in creative style undermines effectiveness, but it also coincides with a decline in favourability among the general public. The shift risks undermining the reputation of the industry as a whole and has implications for its ability to recruit talented and creative people.

82 *The Anatomy of Humbug,* Feldwick, P., Matador, Kibworth Beauchamp, 2015, p106 Feldwick paraphrases Boase, rather than quoting him directly
83 *The Righteous Mind,* p119

The creative scene is fragile
and vulnerable to left-brain
interference

How the advertising brain turned sour: Creativity and Company Culture

The creative scene.

If Florence fostered the humanists of the Renaissance, London was the scene of advertising's golden age in the late 1960s, 1970s and 1980s. It wasn't just a golden age for advertising, but for fashion and popular music too.

There are striking parallels between developments in music of the period and advertising. The Beatles' *Rubber Soul* album had inspired The Beach Boys to create *Pet Sounds*,[84] whose harmonic structures in turn inspired the Beatles in *Sergeant Pepper*. Brian Wilson said of *Rubber Soul*, in a remarkably holistic assessment of the album,

"I liked the way it all went together, the way it was all one thing. It was a challenge to me ... It didn't make me want to copy them but to be as good as them. I didn't want to do the same kind of music, but on the same level."

It was the same in advertising. DDB New York had inspired a new generation of creatives in London to develop their own irreverent style. They didn't want to copy what Bill Bernbach and DDB were doing in New York, but to create great work in a style of their own. London creatives had cognitive diversity; they were coming through from both middle- and working-class backgrounds. This was a time of satire, and work from the London advertising scene found a rich seam in the British class system.[85]

A creative scene emerged, and those who experienced it talk of the excitement for the work and the respect that people had for it.[86] This scene can be said to have had much in common with the Humanists of Florence or the literary salons of 17th-century Paris – an environment of mutual appreciation, where both risk-taking and artful expression are celebrated by the whole group, where amicable competition and encouragement bring the naturally reserved out of their shell. It is what Brian Eno describes as "scenius", where individual talent plays off individual talent to create a kind of "communal genius".[87] It is the very best kind of peer pressure.

This creative scene emerged organically; it owed a great deal to individuals with talent and a shared passion, generous budgets, but also to the supportive environments and people that enabled it to flourish. This kind of community environment – one that cherishes craft and shares a common sensibility – enables the rapid transfer of ideas and great creative leaps. Everyone takes pleasure and an interest in everyone else's work. A protective zone is created around the creatives to allow them to operate. This is precisely the environment in which the right brain blossoms.

But this kind of whole-brained scene is finely balanced and rather fragile, because it relies on individuals' passions and the relationships between them. Difficult to create and vulnerable to interference. It needs to be nurtured and protected by strong characters from the incursions of the left brain.

84 Source 'Surf Music' by Himes, G. *from teachrock.org. Rock and Roll: An American History*
85 See *Stuff from the Loft,* Dave Dye, An interview with Sir Frank Lowe
86 Idem.
87 The creative scene had many of the features of scenius set out in *Scenius, or Communal Genius*, Sterling, B., Wired 2008, and my description here owes much to it

"There are lots of clients who don't have the time to do it properly. The space has been booked before the creative brief has even been written. So they do need a conveyor belt cranking out ads. [...]

And that's okay as long as the ads don't have to do any more than just fill up space. As long as they don't have to achieve any sort of business result. As long as they're being judged on efficiency, not effectiveness."

Dave Trott

The encroaching left brain.

One only need observe split-brain patients to see how the left brain likes to seize control. When split-brain patients, whose *corpus collosum* has lost its inhibitory function through a medical procedure, are asked to arrange patterned cubes so that they form an overall design, the right hand (controlled by the left brain) seeks to take control of the situation. The left brain's attempts to solve the puzzle are hopeless; it cannot work out how to arrange the parts so that they form an overall pattern. When the right hand is restrained, however, and the left hand takes over (controlled by the right brain), the patient sees the big picture within seconds and solves the puzzle with ease.[88] The left brain likes to take control of things even if it doesn't understand them, which means the right brain needs to be given the space and responsibility to operate unencumbered by the left.

There are many contributing factors to the changes in creative style we have witnessed over the last fifteen years. The left-brain pressures brought to bear on agencies by clients and holding companies count among them.

The left brain takes the short view.

Investors are seeking quicker returns today than in the past. It is reported that the average holding time for shares on the world's largest stock exchange has fallen from eight years in 1960 to less than eight months today.[89] With the introduction of quarterly reporting, evidence of 'results' is needed more quickly than ever before. As Gareth Price notes, "80% of CFOs at 400 of the world's largest companies would sacrifice a firm's economic value to meet this quarter's earnings expectations". This leads companies to create advertising that is focused on driving sales volumes by competing on price, and forces companies to cut marketing costs. Return on marketing investment has become a popular (but misguided) means within companies of showing the value of marketing over a short time period, rather than looking at the broader growth picture. There is consequently a new emphasis on 'performance' marketing and channels that can demonstrate any kind of return in the short term. Efficiency over short time periods has trumped effectiveness over the long term. A new *Financial Times* survey in association with the IPA reveals that only two thirds of senior marketers today claim to know how to build and maintain brands.[90] This is a concern when we know that the indirect effects of advertising to a company's stock value far outweigh its direct effects.[91]

88 McGilchrist refers us to Gazzinger, M.S. and LeDoux, J.E., *The Integrated Mind*, Plenum Press, New York 1978
89 See *Thinklong: I believe the future of brands requires collective action to combat short-termism* by Price, G. WARC, 2018. The paper proposes some useful steps to combat short-termism

90 See *The Board-Brand Rift*, a *Financial Times* readership survey in association with and published by the IPA 2019
91 Price refers us to the American Association of Advertising Agencies's finding that advertising affects just 5% of a company's stock value directly but has an indirect effect on 75%

> "Too often you are dealing with the power of people to say 'Maybe'. Great work is bought by powerful people, not by the weak, the ones who say 'maybe', or the ones who hedge their bets."
>
> Sir John Hegarty

The left brain seeks to control.

The *Financial Times* survey examines why clients are moving their budgets away from brand building towards activation, and why they are prioritising the short term. Polling its subscribers, it reveals that 83% believe that their leadership team "believes in a strong brand continually contributing to the bottom line of the business", yet only 37% of subscribers believe that "senior management [in their organisations] rely on the marketing department to deliver powerful creativity and do not get involved", with almost as many, 34%, believing that senior management don't rely on the marketing team and *do get involved*.[92] This should, in theory, make it easier to get 'powerful' advertising signed off, but if creative control is being centralised to the CEO or CFO, then there is a danger that work geared towards the short term – that is more conservative and literal – will be proposed, and that bold brand-building work will be rejected. The *Cadbury's Gorilla* ad (5-Stars, IPA Silver) – now over ten years old – was only aired thanks to the tenacity of then marketing director Phil Rumbol. "Show me a good ad and I'll show you a good client", as Sir Frank Lowe says.[93]

The left brain likes to break things up into smaller parts.

Clients pay agencies differently today. Agencies used to be paid on commission. When creative and media were provided by the same agency, agencies received around 15% commission on gross media costs. This was easy to calculate and administer and meant that both parties were focused on the quality rather than the price of the product. It meant that creative teams had the freedom to think continuously about the client's brand and the work. This changed in the late 1980s when media planning and buying were split out from creative development. Resource package fees (or 'retainer fees') were introduced for agencies in place of commission and now account for around two thirds of all agency agreements. Procurement's left-brain preference for repeatability and process means that fees are now agreed in advance for the year. Retainer fees require client and agency to agree upfront a detailed scope of work and resource plan that will reflect the likely workload of the agency for a defined period. The scope of work shows the different phases of activity required and, against this, the people with the requisite skills and seniority to produce the work. The resulting schedule of people's hours and charge-out rates is translated into a total cost to the client, billable on a monthly basis. Besides covering the agency's staff costs, retainer fees incorporate an allowance for overheads and an allocation for profit.[94]

92 See *The Board-Brand Rift,* 2019. It also reports a worrying perception that 'brand' does not deliver on the priorities of businesses today and cannot help with risk reduction, cashflow or margin
93 See *Stuff from the Loft*, Dave Dye, An interview with Sir Frank Lowe
94 *Agency Remuneration* 2012, IPA, ISBA, MAA and PRCA

"Process is trying to make order out of chaos. Creativity is trying to make chaos to create order. They are at opposite ends of the spectrum."

Sir John Hegarty

This has changed the way that ad agencies work, requiring of them left-brain task focus and attention. The creative's job has been broken down into itemised parts. This inevitably turns creative development into a *process*. Whilst charge-out rates might be appropriate for legal work, one has to ask whether the focused bursts of left-brain attention they require are conducive to creativity. Charge-out rates force creatives to work quickly; they now have only hours rather than weeks to crack a brief. They also work in multiple teams to arrive at more ideas in the timeframe in the hope of striking on a good one. Multiple teams working on one brief doesn't play to the right brain's sense of responsibility, because no one creative team is ultimately responsible for cracking the brief.[95]

In addition to breaking up the work into small parts, procurement departments have been responsible for a steady decline in agency fees over the past twenty years. This makes right-brained advertising less likely, as many of its features incur production costs (actors, sets and costumes). Growing workloads have accompanied this squeeze on costs,[96] with the result that agencies are trapped by low fees, leading to freezes on pay and bonuses, and a reduction in senior talent. Michael Farmer explains:

"Looking at the past ten years, agency workloads have been growing but typical agency fees and headcounts have not. [...] Workloads have been growing on the order of 2-3% on a compounded annual basis, while fees (on a constant dollar basis) have been declining by 2-3% on a compounded annual basis. [...] It only takes fifteen years for an agency's compensation to be cut in half for an equivalent amount of work".[97]

Increased workloads do not help the creative's task. Farmer asserts that:

"Through benign neglect of growing creative workloads, and reluctance to tackle clients over declining client fees, senior agency executives are presiding over the slow decline and over-stretching of a diminishing pool of burned-out creative assets".[98]

---

95 David Abbott warned of the dangers of multiple teams working on the same brief in the mid-1990s in an all-staff memo that re-surfaced recently. Sir Frank Lowe also warns against this practice in his interview with Dave Dye, and intimates that pitching multiple ideas is not the way to create belief in your work. *Stuff from the Loft*, Dave Dye, An interview with Sir Frank Lowe

96 See *Madison Avenue Manslaughter* 2019
97 Idem. p5
98 Idem. p7

Clients are but one of two masters.

"Repeatable methods produce predictable results. This is valuable in manufacturing but not in pursuing creativity."

Martin Weigel

"Rules are what the artist breaks; the memorable never emerged from a formula."

Bill Bernbach

Most advertising agencies today are part of larger publicly listed holding companies and in the period in question, advertising agency acquisitions have intensified.[99] As Sir Frank Lowe[100] explains, when agencies go public, they introduce a third partner into the business; they go from exclusively servicing the client to having to satisfy both client and shareholder. Many agencies today must therefore satisfy both the client's desire for good work and the productivity requirements of their holding companies. Holding companies have continually demanded improved profit performance of their agencies. They have introduced 'stretch targets' and fixed 'staff-cost ratios' that have increased workloads as fees have fallen.[101]

Engineering productivity into a business requires left-brain attention because at the heart of productivity are the instincts of *fixity* and *repeatability*. Companies seek to improve productivity by creating a 'repeatable' business. Repeatability comes from creating and adhering to processes, measuring the results and making incremental improvements, embedding in an organisation what's known as a 'learning culture', whose ultimate goal is to reduce prices. Improvements derived from repetition enable companies to increase their productivity (a greater number of products at lower cost) and reliability. Companies that can achieve these increases in productivity over time are attractive to investors because they demonstrate that the company is getting better at making or selling, with less wasted effort.

The pursuit of the learning curve will help a company increase its output, but it can bring certain dangers in the longer term. A company that pursues a learning-curve strategy will seek to introduce *specialism* within its workforce. Fixed processes and specialism, accompanied by falling prices, can limit a company's ability to behave innovatively, as Ford discovered to its cost in the late 1920s.[102] Ford was ultimately forced to increase its prices.

As Michael Farmer explains, holding companies today "are under threat, and are struggling to maintain their growth rates and profit margins in the face of new competitors (consulting firms), in house agencies and their own understaffed and underpaid agencies".[103]

99 Idem. pp28-38
100 See *Stuff from the Loft*, Dave Dye, An interview with Sir Frank Lowe
101 See *Madison Avenue Manslaughter* 2019, p39
102 See *Limits of the Learning Curve*, Abernathy and Wayne, Harvard Business Review, September 1974 "The heightening rationalization of the process leads

to greater specialization in labor skills and may ultimately lessen workers' pride in their jobs and concern for product quality. Process changes alter the skills requirements from the flexibility of the craftsman to the dexterity of the operative."
103 See *Madison Avenue Manslaughter* 2019, p41
104 See 'How agencies are putting themselves out of business and what we should do about it', Forbes Jan 31 2016

The left brain prizes specialism.

There has been an expansion in the type of work that advertising agencies do today. It used to be relatively simple; they looked after print, radio, outdoor and television. Today they take on a great deal more and are expected to be specialists in social, digital, programmatic, native advertising, influencer and email marketing.[104] Agency specialism has been encouraged by holding companies.[105] Specialism and narrow focus are preferences of the left brain.

But does specialism work in a creative context? A study by business and management professors Taylor and Greve tested the idea of specialism and the industrial learning curve in a creative environment. They studied the collector value of comic books from 234 publishers and 4,485 titles from 1972-1996 alongside their creators' careers. They expected to find a *typical industrial production learning curve.* They hypothesised that creators who made more comics (greater workload) would make better ones. They also believed that the more resources the publisher had (greater publisher size), the better the creators' products would be. Finally, they believed that the more years of experience the creators had (longer tenure), the better their comics would be. They were wrong on all three counts. In fact, a "high-repetition workload negatively impacted performance".[106] What they found was that the more genres (i.e. comedy, crime, fantasy, adult, non-fiction and sci-fi) a creator had worked on, the better. It wasn't so much length as *breadth* of experience that counted. Individual creators with *range* (experience of four or more genres) were more innovative than a team of specialists whose members had collective experience of the same number of genres.[107] The authors conclude that "individuals are capable of more

creative integration of diverse experiences than teams are' and that 'combining knowledge requires a deep understanding of knowledge, rather than information scanning or exposure". For value creation, it pays to expose yourself to a range of inputs and immerse yourself in them.

The need for specialism and speed have encouraged agile working in creative teams, which means that the established art director/copywriter dynamic has been replaced by short-lived 'hot teams' that come together for a given client, project or campaign. The increase in the demand for specialist digital work means that teams will now include a combination of a strategist, data scientist and/or a creative technology expert. Creative teams are now constituted by people who might not know each other and who have narrow specialisms, when it has been shown that teams create better work when their members have *range*, have experience of working together and aren't over worked.[108]

Agency specialisation has, Michael Farmer claims, "limited the technical development of individual agencies and hobbled the intellectual growth of senior client service people".[109] Clients need people who understand the *whole*, rather than one small part of the whole, and specialisation has led to a loss of influence for the senior agency client head with their client. It needn't be so, and indeed this is not the case in management consultancies, where consulting partners are expected to have *range*.

Repeatability and specialism on the one hand (left brain), and novelty and breadth on the other (right brain), are in direct competition with one another, at both a brain-hemisphere and organisational level.[110]

105 See *Madison Avenue Manslaughter* 2019, p34 "WPP's individual companies were specialized and encouraged to stay that way. 'People of specialist skills work best and contribute more when recruited, trained and inspired by specialist companies', stated WPP's 2003 Annual Report."
106 See *Range*, pp 208-210

107 Idem. Epstein refers us to Taylor, A., and Greve, H. R., 'Superman or Fantastic Four? Knowledge Combination and Experience in Innovative Teams', *Academy of Management Journal* 49, no.4 (2006): 723-40
108 See Taylor, A., and Greve, H. R., 'Superman or Fantastic Four? Knowledge Combination and Experience in Innovative Teams', 2006

109 See *Madison Avenue Manslaughter* 2019, pp 90-92
110 *Limits of the Learning Curve*, Abernathy and Wayne, Idem. "The unfortunate implication is that product innovation is the enemy of cost efficiency, and vice versa."

"When you start working on a job for a client, no one knows where the answer will come from and how that idea – which may not conform to the brief's assumptions about what is required – could actually transform that client's business."

Sir John Hegarty

The left brain likes to standardise: the global ad.

The tendency of the holding company is to standardise and centralise. Holding companies have used their scale to sell themselves as global partners to global clients, and together with clients, they have sought to reduce costs through standardisation, leading to the 'global ad'. The global ad presents a problem for creative teams, because many of the right-brain features they rely on are no longer possible. Accents, dialogue and wordplay become very difficult, and local cultural references or personalities are almost out of the question. Characters and drama ('a scene unfolding') is also difficult to pull off; people can feel more like two-dimensional cutouts, and a sense of betweenness is lost. A sense of place disappears, and the advertising starts to feel dislocated from reality. Language is reduced to a tool rather than a means of expression. As Sir John Hegarty has observed, visual techniques are proposed as a substitute for an idea, in the hope that this will make it easier to gain approval across many different regional stakeholders.[111] Adrian Holmes cites Simon Clift, who referred to "bad global advertising as being like the CNN weather forecast for the world".[112] Advertising that is intended for everyone can end up being entertaining to almost nobody. It is, of course, possible to work within these constraints. The IPA award-winning global Snickers ad, featuring Rowan Atkinson as Mr Bean, is a good example of how you can create work that connects with audiences across the world. But the loss of the right-brain features we are seeing in advertising must surely be a direct consequence, in no small part, of the centralised global ad.

The left brain abstracts.

There is little doubt that today advertising is subject to much greater left-brain scrutiny than it was in the 1980s. The left brain likes to think in the abstract, divorce things from their context for analysis, and all too often advertising strategy is deemed more important than the potential of the work itself to transform a business. 'Yes, but does it meet the brief?' seems to be a question used early in the development process, as Sir John Hegarty suggests, to dismiss an idea.[113] The left brain chops off anything it doesn't like, and this is a question that seeks to discount anything distinctive or entertaining, with a flattening effect on work. The brief is only one of many routes to a creative solution to the business problem. In an analytical, linear process it becomes *the* route. 'Should the brief be re-examined in light of the idea?' should perhaps be the right brain's answer. *Ideas about the thing have become more important than the thing itself.* The result is advertising where strategy is often all too clearly visible in the work.

Digital guidelines favour left-brain features.

It is estimated that over a half of all agency revenues (US) are from 'digital work'.[114] The advent of social media platforms over the time period in question has given advertisers a new way to target people. These platforms have developed guidelines for how advertisers should use them by establishing the kind of advertising that works in the short term. Balancing the user experience with the need for advertising is a difficult business and the guidelines tend to encourage shorter time spots, breaking longer ads into shorter parts and splitting the screen into multiple images. They encourage a single message, showing your brand upfront and getting in close on your product. They also tend to promote visual rhythm and repetition. Guidelines such as these promote the use of left-brain features in advertising, which, as we have seen, don't elicit a positive emotional response. Features such as abstraction, repetition and rhythmic devices will lower your chances of long-term growth. With companies increasingly designing for mobile first, before considering TV or other channels, these guidelines are harmful to the long-term growth prospects of brands operating across channels.

Caught in one mind, not two.

As we saw in Section 3, success in advertising relies on the unique capabilities of the right brain to entertain and connect with its audiences, to be alert to new ideas, to reference the past and its culture, to portray people as they interact in context, to play with ambiguity, contradiction, metaphor and humour. Cultural changes within clients and agencies have led to the introduction of practices that assume advertising operates like manufacturing; practices that have embraced the power of the fixed ratio and the principles of productivity. The left-brain instincts of centralisation and standardisation are behind these changes. The left brain believes that creativity is linear, can be mapped out from beginning to end, with pre-determined inputs and outputs.

We would expect, in this drive for repeatability, productivity and scale, to see left-brain attentional preferences emerging among clients and practitioners, because the left brain is better suited to achieving these goals.

111 See *Hegarty on Advertising*, pp 188-189
112 Adrian Holmes, Former Chief Creative Officer Worldwide for Lowe and D&AD President, interview with Victoria Andrews for Unilever in-house magazine, October 2002 on *Stuff from the Loft*

113 See *Hegarty on Advertising*, pp 79
114 See 'State of the agency world: Digital rules, growth slows, consultancies surge', AdAge, April 30, 2018

Left-brain instincts in media and advertising agencies.

Two studies by Reach Solutions (formerly TrinityMirror Solutions) and house51 show that those working in **media** and **advertising** today have thinking styles that are markedly more analytical, categorical and individualistic than the general populace – that they have a natural preference for a left-brain thinking style.

In *Why We Shouldn't Trust Our Gut Instinct*,[115] Tenzer and Murray point to how those working in **media agencies** today are much younger (84% media vs 35% modern mainstream are aged 18-40) and much more likely to have a degree than the modern mainstream (while less than a third of the general public has a degree, it is a basic recruitment requirement in agencies). This is bound to influence how they think about the world, and indeed the authors show that those working in agencies place greater value on power and achievement (the left-brain characteristics of control and goal attainment) than the general public, and that they mistakenly assume that these are values shared by the modern mainstream. In a repeat of a classic Kahneman study, those working in agencies were much more likely to say that it was fair for a hardware store that had been selling snow shovels for £15 to raise its price to £20 the morning after a large snowstorm. They were happier to embrace modern economic theory than the general public was, leading the authors to conclude that agencies are "out of touch with what real people thought was 'fair'". This is noteworthy because the right brain has been shown to play an important role in "mediating an egalitarian attitude - i.e. the promotion of equality and fairness in the distribution of resources".[116] In another experiment, the authors asked respondents to say whether a panda or a banana went better with a monkey, showing all three lined up together. Those working in agencies were more likely to put the panda with the monkey – that's to say, to group the items by *category*, just as the left brain would – than the general public, who were more likely to associate bananas with the monkey. In another question, respondents were asked how happy a person was when shown at the centre of a group of other people. Facial expressions of the central figure and those around her were changed. The judgement of those working in agencies of the central figure was less affected by her social context; they were more focused on the individual than the contextual cues – they were less likely to 'see the whole' than the modern mainstream. The authors also ran psychological profiling, revealing that those working in agencies were more likely to think they had personal control over the events in their lives and felt a greater need for recognition than the general public, broadly mapping to left-brain instincts.

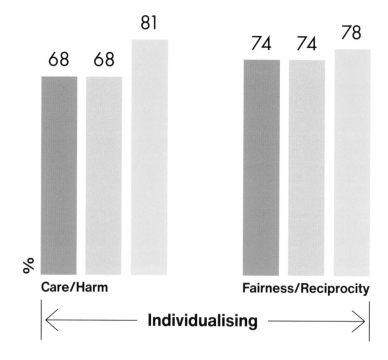

Those working in media agencies today are, therefore, more likely to display a preference for left-brain attention than the mainstream populace – an *analytical* rather than a *holistic* view of the world. The authors conclude of those working in media agencies that, "the implicit impact of their economic, cultural and professional environment constantly pulls them closer to the linear, analytic end of the thinking spectrum".

The social, educational and cultural make-up of those working across advertising and media is very similar, so these left-brain instincts are likely to be shared by advertising agencies. Indeed, more recent work by Reach Solutions and house51 confirms that **a similar gap exists between advertising agencies and those in the modern mainstream**.[117] Using Jonathan Haidt's moral-foundations framework, they assess the moral values of those working in advertising agencies today and, again, compare them with the modern mainstream.

Haidt's framework describes five moral foundations, which can be split into two broad groups: those that promote the welfare and rights of the individual – care and fairness ('individualising'), and those that promote the ethics of community – loyalty, authority and sanctity ('binding'). Haidt describes these five moral foundations as 'taste buds', and asserts that, as Western societies have become more educated, rich and democratic, the minds of its intellectuals have changed, becoming more focused on just two of these: care and fairness. "They became more analytic and less holistic";[118] terms which have considerable overlap with

115 See *Why We Shouldn't Trust Our Gut Instinct*, Tenzer A. and Murray, I., whitepaper by Reach Solutions and house51, 2019
116 See 'Cerebral Lateralization of Pro- and Anti-Social Tendencies', Hecht, D., in *Experimental Neurobiology,* March 2014

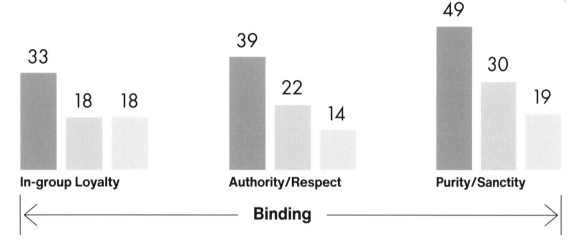

Fig 49 The industry has different ethical and cultural settings from the modern mainstream.
'Creatives' data was subsequently shared by the author on Twitter
(The labels are the authors' own) Source: *The Empathy Delusion*, Tenzer and Murray

Modern Mainstream
Marketing & Advertising
Creatives (art and copywriting)

33   18   18
In-group Loyalty

39   22   14
Authority/Respect

49   30   19
Purity/Sanctity

Binding

McGilchrist's description of the instincts of the left (analytic) and right (holistic) brain. In other words, they have lost three taste receptors.

Tenzer and Murray show that this is true of those working in advertising and marketing (and particularly of creatives), who are much less likely than the modern mainstream to place a value on 'binding' moral foundations, through a study designed to ascertain how much they agree with questions that meet the criteria of these foundations.

Those familiar with Haidt's work will know it asserts that those on the political left are much less likely to place value on the 'binding' foundations, whereas those on the political right place value on all of them. Those working in advertising are more likely to have left-wing political affiliations, as Tenzer and Murray's study shows, but what's striking is that *regardless* of political preferences, those working in **marketing and advertising agencies reject binding ethics more than the modern mainstream.**

This has important implications for the type of work that is made. For one thing, it tells us that, while those working in marketing believe that people want to *stand out*, the modern mainstream actually places a much greater value on *fitting in*, as the authors put it. It may be that those working in advertising agencies have always had a different outlook from the mainstream – had less respect for authority, for instance. But taken together, the findings of these studies suggest that those working in media and advertising

agencies today are less holistic and associative – less 'right brained' – in their outlook, that they are more individualistic and that they place less value on the ethics of community and tradition, than the mainstream. They are more *analytical*, something that has been encouraged by the holding companies.[119] This means that they will miss many of the things the right brain – and the general public – prizes. To borrow Haidt's metaphor, it is as if advertisers and agencies only have two of the required taste buds needed to delight their diners. If the food they prepare for their guests tastes bland, it is because the right-brain ingredients of characters, betweenness, dialogue, the implicit and a clear sense of time and place have been left at the back of the cupboard.

This disconnect between what is prized by the industry and what entertains the public is evidenced by System1's testing. Whilst Cannes Gold Lions tend to test well, nearly a half of the ads that are the most prized by the industry for their creativity – that win a Cannes Grand Prix – achieve only 1-Star when tested among the public.[120] As Tenzer and Murray conclude, advertising and marketing need to embrace the ethics of community to connect with audiences because "tradition, group loyalty and sanctity [...] remain relevant for the mainstream". We need to close the gap in outlook between advertising practitioners and the general public to create effective advertising. Greater moral and cognitive range is needed among those working in advertising – we need to "broaden the palate", as Haidt puts it.

117 *The Empathy Delusion*, Tenzer A. and Murray, I., whitepaper by Reach Solutions and house51, 2019
118 *The Righteous Mind*, pp131-149, in particular p141
119 See *Madison Avenue Manslaughter* 2019, p87

120 Results presented at Cannes 2019. See
www.campaignlive.co.uk/article/cannes-grand-prix-winners-less-likely-resonate-emotionally/1587624

"The brief is nothing but a piece of paper
that has been crafted by
someone who all too often wants to
try to close and, sadly, control the
process. I'm always trying to open up the
process, not close it down.
I don't want to be controlled:
I want to be liberated."

Sir John Hegarty

From culture to practice.

A shift in culture therefore needs to take place, but it also pays, in today's context, to reflect on the *practice* of creating work.

Putting creative development *right*.

How might we maximise our chances of creating entertaining work that drives growth over the long term? What would right-brained briefing and working practices look and feel like? Is there anything we can learn from successful working practices of the past to create more entertaining work today? The following draws principally on the documented experiences of the late and supremely talented creative director John Webster and those he worked with, compiled by Sarah Carter.[121] John Webster's work connected with audiences; ten of the top 100 greatest ads as voted for by the British public were created by him.[122] The following also references the documented experiences of Sir Frank Lowe, Sir John Hegarty and Adrian Holmes.[123] It has benefited from discussions with Sarah Carter, Paul Feldwick, Adrian Holmes and many others.

Brief so the right brain can hear you.

The client brief needs to be clear, and the creative brief liberating. The right brain understands things as they really are, in the embodied world, rather than the represented world of the left brain at one step removed. It listens out for little 'burrs', as Sarah Carter puts it, that stick to your clothes; words, phrases and sounds that immediately present a scenario, that have an in-built ambiguity or that sound contradictory. It listens for idioms and metaphors. The point of the creative brief is to get the ball rolling, and important words and phrases are much more likely to come out in chance conversation. This is what BMP used to call 'narrative creative briefing'. The planners wrote just a couple of paragraphs outlining the important points on a piece of paper – a useful prompt to take into the creative briefing session – around which they could have a free-flowing conversation.[124]

Planner Jon Steel learned the difficulties of creative briefing the hard way. He was working with creative director John Webster and had the task of preparing a creative brief for him. Jon had prepared a careful piece of strategic thinking

121 See Sarah Carter's internal DDB publication, *John Webster. The Earth People's Ad Man*, which deserves broader publication
122 Carter references *100 Greatest TV Ads*, Sunday Times and Channel 4, 2000

on the young British beer drinker, which he tried to take Webster through. John said, "Just talk to me. Talk to me about these blokes. Without any of the intellectual stuff". They talked for an hour and at the end, John said, "That was useful". A phrase Jon had used in conversation had reminded Webster of a scene in a film, which made him think of what a beer drinker would do if placed within that film – a character and a scenario that led to an idea. As Jon Steel remarks,

"I realised that it was much more important to be useful than clever. It wasn't even my job to have ideas – rather to create an environment where others were more likely to have them, and feel comfortable expressing them". [125]

It was listening for these little burrs that led to the Honey Monster. Webster thought it was interesting that mothers referred to their children as 'little monsters'. On another occasion, in the days when most households had milk delivered to their door, the planner working on the Unigate account explained to Webster that 'housewives' of the time couldn't understand why they were always running out of milk. It was this conversational way of framing the problem that gave Webster the idea of the milk-stealing Humphries. The right brain has a good eye and a good ear for a memorable turn of phrase. It's important to play to it.

Keep the idea in the living right brain; don't represent or abstract it.

The 'burr' can be easily lost. It's important not to overthink it, to seek to reduce it, and don't abstract it; try instead to build on it and add depth to it. Writing things out in words (the left brain's domain) can sometimes have a deadening effect, so think of how you might convey it so simply that a child would understand it; do the gestures, actions, sounds and voices. Don't try to describe it; act it instead. Webster spoke to anyone and everyone about his characters and ideas, trying them out on people who didn't work in advertising. Use your influences and sources to bring it to life for people, "she'd look a bit like this, and sound like this, and say this whenever..." Get people to feel it.

123 In addition to Dave Dye's excellent interviews with advertising luminaries on *Stuff from the Loft*, I also draw on *Hegarty on Advertising*, by Sir John Hegarty.
124 John Webster. *The Earth People's Ad Man*, p 41
125 John Webster. *The Earth People's Ad Man*, pp 27-29

Establishing a backstory encourages you to create a scenario, develop dialogue and introduce a foil
— essential for establishing a right-brained sense of time, place and betweenness.

It's a right-brained craft, not a left-brained profession.

A craftsman patiently accumulates learned experience over time and follows their instinct, whereas a professional follows procedure and rules. Creating remarkable work means going to extraordinary lengths, and, as Sir John Hegarty says, *putting something of yourself into it*,[126] not following rigid procedure.

Webster displayed this craft in his advertising characters. Characters offer the opportunity to portray product qualities through people – the right brain's way of seeing the world. They also give a campaign longevity (we will return to the importance of characters in section 5). Webster had a highly developed sense for the living and the implicit, which meant he could imbue his characters with a distinctive and memorable quiddity. He also had *curiosity and range*.

To create something new, it pays to put your right brain in the way of wonderful things. Webster hoarded funny sayings, gestures, anecdotes, drawings and music – he created a secret library of the right brain. He would use these things when trying to bring his embryonic ideas to life for his colleagues.

The idea of the Cresta bear came from a film John had seen, called *Taking Off*, and specifically the hippy boyfriend of the runaway daughter. The idea came to him of a rebellious teenage bear who had left home because he couldn't face the taste of seawater anymore. The appearance of the bear itself was inspired by James Thurber's line-drawing cartoons. The bear's twitch 'spasm' brought on by the milky carbonated soft drink, was inspired by Jack Nicholson's character in *Easy Rider* who, on being released from the police station, takes a swig of whiskey and then exclaims "Yaah, nick, nick, nick, fa, fa, fa, kaagh!" with accompanying chicken-wing arm movement.[127]

Webster thought it important to create a backstory for his characters and would even write biographies for them for clients. He created one for the Honey Monster, whose ancestors had evolved from small honey-loving creatures on a remote desert island to be tall enough to reach the honey from the trees. One day a bachelor in the Navy, called Henry (played by Henry McGee), found the Honey Monster and brought him home to live with him. The Honey Monster thought of him as his Mummy, hence the line, "Tell them about the Honey, Mummy". Fleshing out a character like this allows you to create depth – a backstory that the general public can never know for sure, but that their right brains will implicitly sense and fill in from what they see, and the more they can fill in the implicit backstory themselves, the better. Establishing a backstory encourages you to create a scenario, develop dialogue and even introduce a foil – very important for establishing a right-brained sense of time, place and betweenness. It helps you to stay true to your character too; Webster was always very clear about what the Honey Monster would or wouldn't do.[128]

126 *Hegarty on Advertising*, Sir John Hegarty,
Thames & Hudson 2017
127 *John Webster. The Earth People's Ad Man*, pp22-26
128 *John Webster. The Earth People's Ad Man*, pp40-45
129 Idem. p67

The right brain understands the living and the implicit.

For his Smash Martians ads, Webster obtained the services of Peter Hawkins, who did the voices of children's television characters Zippy, Captain Pugwash and the Daleks. John knew that voices are very important (he would ask his planner to say the word 'crunch' repeatedly in his Lancastrian accent, just because he loved the way it sounded). When it came to the Cresta bear, Webster involved the imposing Canadian Thick Wilson to do the bear's voice. He also commissioned the best animator in Richard Williams (who animated *The Pink Panther* and later *Who framed Roger Rabbit*) to draw the bear. Williams knew his craft and knew he had to order a special pencil from Germany for the drawings.

He succeeded in getting the appearance and movement of the bear, including his distinctive 'spasm', just right. He even engineered visual depth into a character that was, to all intents and purposes, a simple line drawing.

When it came to the Hofmeister Bear, John knew just how important the bear's walk was, explaining, "Laurence Olivier always said he knew when he'd got the character when he got the walk right. With George, when we got the walk right, it kind of gave him a swagger, 'I'm Jack the lad'."[129] These embodied ticks and mannerisms are what make characters feel real and distinctive.

Inspiration [can be] indirectly courted by using chance as a way to limit the power of conscious intention."

Iain McGilchrist

The left brain likes things to be fixed and unchanging; the right brain favours flow and spontaneity.

Right-brained flow over left-brain fixity.

As McGilchrist explains, creativity is a journey of discovery not an invention. It's very tempting once you have arrived at an idea to stick rigidly to it, even in the face of negative feedback. The left brain likes things to be fixed and unchanging, but the right brain favours flow and spontaneity. Go with the right brain's sense of flow; arriving at the best work means accepting that it can be improved at every stage.

BMP put all animatics into research, and it was feedback from the general public, describing how they felt about the idea, that helped Webster to rework the Honey Monster. In research, children had reacted badly to an early small version of the Honey Monster because monsters are meant to be enormous and smash the place up a bit; mums didn't like it because it acted like a badly behaved child. So Webster turned the idea upside down, and made the monster huge and rather clumsy. This made the monster endearing rather than bad, and an instant success.

Webster had a very healthy view of research, and "believed research was data not a decision. He would look at the failings exposed by research and try to overcome them", explains Alfredo Marcantonio.[130] Eliciting emotional response to advertising early in the process helps to focus development on the right-brain features that matter; it prevents the excesses of the left brain from destroying a good idea.

BBDO used System1's testing to identify their *Basketball* ad for Guinness as the most engaging of six scripts, by testing in animatic form. *Basketball* was part of the *Made of More* campaign that would go on to win an IPA Gold Award. It

places a strong emphasis on in-group loyalty. The animatic of the ad – a roughly drawn version of the ad with the intended voiceover and music – used voiceover from beginning to end. Knowing that voiceover (unilateral communication – left brain) dampens emotional response, System1 proposed removing the voiceover and testing it again. The version with no voiceover resulted in a better score – enough to give the agency and client confidence to reduce the voiceover in the final cut and let the ad breathe. The final cut tested as a 5-Star ad and was part of a campaign that helped Guinness restore its market share in the UK and Ireland.[131] Research can be used to experiment with new ideas and have results back within hours today.

Research can also be used to draw out advertising styles that work well. A meta-analysis of System1's emotional testing of IKEA's ads for Mother helped them to identify the strength of surreal characters in real settings across their evolving *Wonderful Everyday* campaign. As the author of the IPA paper describes, "We found our strongest results came from injecting the surreal into real life; whilst the everyday was something that IKEA paid great attention to, consumers didn't – glimpses of the surreal helped transform the everyday from the humdrum it represented and drove spikes in happiness."[132] With hindsight it's clear that the success of 'surreal characters in real settings' is down to the right brain's appreciation of characters in a clearly defined place. The campaign won an IPA Silver.

Research needs to be used carefully, however, because all too often conceptual left-brain measures are interpreted and used by the left brain in such a way that they destroy an ad. System1 has seen a telling example of this. The original edit of an ad with right-brain betweenness (depicting a mother and her young daughter in a heart-warming, touching conversation) was rather unsympathetically recut based on recommendations of left-brained market research.

130 Idem. p57
131 See IPA Paper in *Advertising Works* 23: IPA Effectiveness Awards 2016. London: WARC and System1, *Unlocking Profitable Growth*, Kearon, Ewing and Wood 2017
132 See IPA Paper in *Advertising Works* 24: IPA Effectiveness Awards 2018 London: WARC

The recommendations resulted in a version with brighter lighting, a rhythmic soundtrack and a much diminished sense of betweenness. System1's post-testing of the two ads revealed a drop of nearly a whole Star rating for the final edit – the version that sadly the client had already decided to air.

Then there are happy accidents. Serendipity has created some of the most enduring advertising moments. During the filming of the final scene of the original *Smash Martians* ad, in the scene where the Martians are laughing at human stupidity, one of the robots by chance fell over backwards as it bobbed up and down. The right brain interprets this as the Martian having fallen about laughing – how very human! – making the ad even funnier. In another of Webster's ads for Hellmann's mayonnaise, Geoffrey Palmer sits next to a live rabbit as they both contemplate an undressed salad. The script suggested the rabbit should be alert, but the rabbit was rather nonchalant, and his ears lay flat. In one lucky take, something startled the rabbit, causing it to turn towards Palmer at exactly the right time with its ears pricked up.[133] The ad went on to win a Cannes Grand Prix. This would be done using CGI today and would be much less effective for it.

In the Cinzano ads featuring Leonard Rossiter and Joan Collins, it was Leonard Rossiter's suggestion on set that they try the old 'What's the time?' music-hall routine.[134] Joan Collins tipping her drink over herself was forever after the basis of the Cinzano ads they worked on together. In the same way, Rowan Atkinson took it upon himself to improve many of the scripts for his Barclaycard ads.[135] Acting is an embodied craft and good actors will know instinctively what will make any scene work better. Trust them to help you.

Direction too, of course, is supremely important. When working on Courage's *Gertcha* ad, Webster worked with director, Hugh Hudson. Hudson suggested to Webster that they use award-winning cinematographer Robert Krasker. Krasker had worked on *Brief Encounter* but had by this point retired. He was a master of black and white cinematography. Hudson contended that a younger director simply wouldn't have had the right experience to do it. Webster thought it was an excellent idea and agreed. Krasker lit the scene for them; the lighting seemed worryingly stark on the set, but the effect on black and white film was superb.[136]

Many important improvements take place, therefore, between the script and the final film. The script, storyboard or animatic should not be viewed as a 'legal document', as Webster put it, but as a 'start point'. Dave Trott expresses it beautifully when he reflects on what John taught him,

"For John, the script was the start of the process. The brief for a commercial. After that everything began to come to life. Everything was an opportunity to make it better. For surprises to happen. Choosing a director, casting the actors, looking at the sets, choosing the music, the VO, the editing, the grading, the typography, the performances. For me the script was a straitjacket. For John it was a springboard".[137]

The 'validated storyboard' has acquired a quasi-legal status, but it should always be the basis for something better. It's in clients' interests to allow happy accidents to occur and to allow actors and directors to bring their craft to the ad.

Leaving room for serendipity and spontaneity is how you hit upon something truly special. Without it, we would have no Dulux dog, and nor would Kubrick have set *2001: A Space Odyssey* to Strauss's *Zarathustra*. Genius occurs in the doing, not the planning.

133 *John Webster. The Earth People's Ad Man*, pp 37-38
134 *Stuff from the Loft,* An interview with Sir Frank Lowe, by Dave Dye
135 See 'A True Story: The Birth of a Great Campaign', Paul Feldwick, in *Market Leader*, Issue 31, Winter 2005, pp 30-33
136 *John Webster. The Earth People's Ad Man*, pp 51-55
137 *John Webster. The Earth People's Ad Man*, pp 48

The left brain does language; the right brain does music.

It helps to think of music early on in development. Music has a real bearing on how people feel towards an ad. System1 has seen different music tracks on the same ad make the difference between a 3-Star and a 5-Star performance. Music is not something that should be tackled as an afterthought because it can change your entire direction of travel and put a completely different complexion on an idea. In fact, it can form the basis of the idea. Webster's Trio and Kia Ora ads are excellent examples of how the music can be the start point for an idea. These ads would not be possible without the underlying track.

Music can also work to communicate a recurring device, just as Bach's Air from *Orchestral Suite no.3* did for Hamlet Cigars or the re-orchestrated Robert Palmer's *Johnny and Mary* track for the *Papa Nicole* Renault Clio ads. It also helps people to interpret what's happening as a scene unfolds, saying something about the relationship between characters and conveying a sense of time and place.

In Hovis' Boy on a Bike ad (1973, recently re-mastered and re-aired), the Ashington Colliery brass band was invited to play a transcription of Dvořak's *New World Symphony*. Northern brass bands use cornets rather than trumpets and so provide a more mournful sound.[138] That it is played by a brass band immediately conveys a sense of place, tradition and of time having passed – a sense of immediate nostalgia. The ad is as powerful today as it was then, exhibiting nearly every one of the right-brain features identified in section 3, achieving 5-Stars in testing and putting it ahead of 99% of ads made and aired today.

Harmony and timbre are the aural equivalent of visual depth. Highly rhythmic soundtracks, the preference of the left brain, are less likely to trigger a positive emotional response and lack the depth required to convey meaning at a meta level.

Encounters with the left brain.

The left brain can only say yes or no to what is presented to it by the right brain, so what should you do when your work comes up against the left brain? There are a few ways you can tackle this.

The first is to invite the doubtful party to watch other people reacting to the work. This is what Phil Rumbol did with *Cadbury's Gorilla*. He made copies of the ad for his colleagues and asked them to take it home with them over the weekend to show their families. It had the desired effect for the *Cadbury's Gorilla* ad, but it's a high-risk strategy and doesn't always work.

The second is not to play its game. When the marketing director of Cresta asked John Webster, "But why on earth is there a polar bear in it?" John simply replied, "Why not?" You can also flip the risk around the other way. It's easier to justify and articulate a flat, left-brained idea than it is a right-brained one, even though the lost upside to the business can be enormous. It is the left-brained course of action that instead needs to be questioned. Sir Frank Lowe would sometimes say to clients, "Are you confident, knowing that in turning this down, and in going with something else, your business will be less successful as a result?"[139] Draw on your right brain's acting abilities and speak with energy, spontaneity, empathy and humour to sell your creative idea.

Finally, knowing that the ad stands a good chance of creating long-term growth is helpful. Margaret Burke, once marketing director at 3, said to System1 in relation to their 5-Star *Pony* ad, that emotional testing with a hardwired link to effectiveness had "helped us to be brave, without being stupidly brave". CMO Jon Evans was able to make a similar argument for his work at Lucozade Suntory to his senior stakeholders. There is great merit in being able to show the likely long-term effects of an ad in the future, before you air it.

Section 4
Summary.

1 A creative scene is dependent on people, their relationships and a common sensibility; it is fragile and vulnerable to left-brain interference. It needs to be adequately funded, nurtured and protected.

2 Client decision-making today is shorter-term, more centralised and there is a changing client base that favours short-term marketing strategies.

3 Procurement's left-brain instincts have made the creative's task harder: breaking the creative's task up into smaller parts, introducing processes and a downward pressure on agency fees.

4 Pressures on agencies from advertising holding companies to increase their profitability have ushered in staff-cost ratios, reduced 'heads' and increased workloads.

5 Agencies are expected to be specialists in an ever-wider range of marketing fields. Specialism has been encouraged at an agency and creative-team level. 'Hot teams' comprised of specialists – who don't always know each other – are brought together for a project; yet creativity requires people with range, who know each other, with enough time to immerse themselves in the brief.

6 Standardisation in the form of 'the global ad' makes it very difficult to create right-brained advertising.

7 Guidelines from social-media platforms promote abstraction and rhythmic devices, features of the left brain. These practices are being adopted in work intended for other channels, such as TV.

8 The economic, cultural and professional environment of agencies today requires a linear, analytical, left-brain thinking style.

9 A gap has emerged between the thinking styles and values of agency employees and those of the general public; agencies mistakenly project their own values and preferences on to their audiences.

10 We can improve our chances of achieving entertaining and emotional work through right-brained briefing and working practices, seeking to improve on the work at every stage.

11 Testing geared towards the long term can help to create more emotional work and give confidence in its long-term effects.

In the next section, we will point towards advertising styles that lead to sustained growth over the long term, and also touch upon those that are intrinsically short term in nature.

138 See *Stuff from the Loft,* Dave Dye, An interview with Sir Frank Lowe
139 Idem.

Entertain for commercial gain

Towards a more effective creative style:
Creativity for Growth

Entertain for long-term growth.

The right brain empathises, can see things from two perspectives, appreciates metaphor and humour, and the sublime through awe. These things give us a sense of perspective on the world; they also make for very successful advertising.

System1's testing, informed by Paul Ekman's work, identifies twelve different types of happiness that might be elicited by an ad: amusement, awe, contentment, ecstasy/bliss, excitement, being pleased for others, pride, relief, gratitude, sensorial pleasure, *Schadenfreude* and upliftment. The question works as follows: anyone who has said the ad has made them feel happy is asked a further question to ascertain which, if any, of these types of happiness is felt (multiple answers are possible). Overlaying these scores on to the IPA Effectiveness Databank helps us to establish the types of happiness associated with very large business effects.

The table below shows the strongest and weakest ads on each type of happiness (high vs low incidence) against the business effects achieved for each group. Ads that elicit *Schadenfreude*, amusement, awe upliftment or ecstasy/bliss have a greater association with the very large business effects categories used by the IPA (profit gain, share gain, penetration gain, price-sensitivity reductions or loyalty).

Let's examine the types of happiness that are most associated with business effects in the light of what we know about the right brain.

Schadenfreude.

Schadenfreude, **or 'joy in others' misfortune'** as it is described in System1's testing, is not a common response – System1 rarely sees more than 10% of those feeling happy selecting it and some care needs to be taken in its interpretation. The way the question is asked (a follow-up question for those indicating the ad made them happy) and the context of its use (in relation to advertising) means that respondents by and large interpret the term positively. The context in which it is selected is usually a humorous rather than a cruel one: there is a significant correlation between the presence of *Schadenfreude* and amusement across System1's testing. It is more typically born of a sense of empathy with the characters involved: the bringing down of hubris or folly, tendencies that the self-aware see in themselves from time to time. It's the kind of humour that you would encounter in Moliere's *Tartuffe*, the pricking of Mr Pooter's aspirations in *The Diary of a Nobody* or Captain Mainwaring's pomposity in *Dad's Army*. For *Schadenfreude* here, therefore, read a corrective 'comeuppance'.

Schadenfreude as we describe it here, then, is felt in relation to advertising that shows human excesses brought low, rather than irresponsible cruelty or gloating. To illustrate the measure in action, let's compare scores between VW's *Laughing Horses* ad (5-Star) and Harvey Nichols *Spent it on Myself* Christmas campaign (1-Star). The VW ad depicts the difficulties a non-VW driver has reverse parking his car and horsebox, much to the amusement of onlooking horses, who are bent double

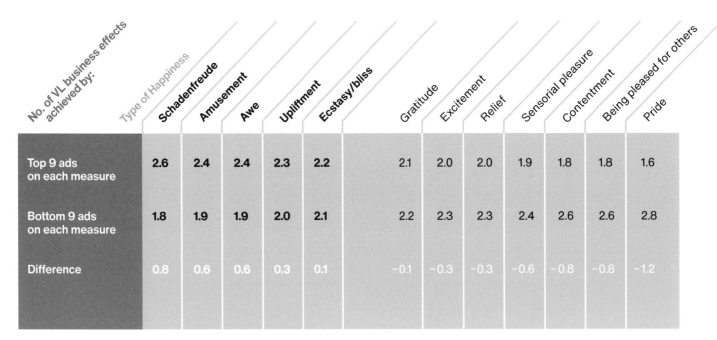

No. of VL business effects achieved by: / Type of Happiness	Schadenfreude	Amusement	Awe	Upliftment	Ecstasy/bliss	Gratitude	Excitement	Relief	Sensorial pleasure	Contentment	Being pleased for others	Pride
Top 9 ads on each measure	2.6	2.4	2.4	2.3	2.2	2.1	2.0	2.0	1.9	1.8	1.8	1.6
Bottom 9 ads on each measure	1.8	1.9	1.9	2.0	2.1	2.2	2.3	2.3	2.4	2.6	2.6	2.8
Difference	0.8	0.6	0.6	0.3	0.1	–0.1	–0.3	–0.3	–0.6	–0.8	–0.8	–1.2

Fig 50 The relationship between different types of happiness and very large business effects

with laughter. It achieves high levels of amusement (61% of the sample), high levels of Schadenfreude (21%) and no contempt (0%). The *Spent it on Myself* ad seeks to shock by depicting people opening low-outlay Christmas presents from Harvey Nichols because, as the gift giver explains to the recipient, the gift giver has spent the money on themselves instead.

This ad achieves low levels of amusement (17%) and lower still levels of Schadenfreude (5%), but high levels of contempt (11%). Note how *Spent it on Myself's* individualistic tone strikes at the heart of nearly all of Haidt's moral foundations – in-group loyalty and sanctity, certainly, but even fairness and care. We will return to advertising's desire to shock later.

The right brain is involved in mediating empathy, whereas the left brain is involved in mediating anti-social emotions and mental states, such as gloating or justification of a crime.[140] System1's measure of *Schadenfreude* hints at empathy and self-awareness, at proportion and perspective, rather than outright meanness. For long and broad effects, play to the empathy and self-awareness of the right brain. The right brain is what helps us to see ourselves as a person like others, as McGilchrist explains, and playing to this can make for very entertaining advertising.

The right brain is what helps us to understand whether someone is lying or not and distinguishes jokes from lies.

Amusement.

Most humour is dependent on the right brain's ability to see the relations between things, to see something from two different perspectives, to see that a thing and its opposite can both simultaneously be true. As McGilchrist explains, it is the right hemisphere that helps us to understand 'the moral of a story' or 'the point of a joke', as studies have shown.[141] It understands the meaning of a whole phrase in context. It can understand what's implied, appreciate vocal nuance and perceives the shifts in emphasis that can completely change the meaning of a phrase. On the other hand, study of patients with right-brain lesions has revealed that the left brain can only understand explicit meaning. Irony and sarcasm rely on the right brain – an understanding of intonation and context that reveals that someone in fact really means the exact opposite of what they are saying. The right hemisphere is what helps us to understand whether someone is lying or not and distinguishes jokes from lies.

Le Trèfle's 5-Star *Emma* toilet paper ad is the most amusing ad System1 has tested to date. It uses many of the right-brain features we saw in Section 3 – dialogue, characters with agency, a sense of betweenness and lived time. It also uses dramatic irony – the audience can see that the husband is annoying the long-suffering wife throughout (it relies on the right brain to interpret Emma's facial features) and that the husband lacks the self-awareness to see it. It pokes fun at the consistency, rigidity and self-importance of the husband's rather left-brained behaviour with its superb pay-off. This ad was highly successful for Le Trèfle. It led to a run on the product and its international fame helped the company to gain distribution in new markets.

So humour is an important – perhaps the most important – tool in the creative's armoury. It enables you to reach the parts that more literal communication simply can't reach. Moreover, it suggests that the advertiser has a right-brained human intelligence and so renders everything they do and say more plausible. It helps you to connect and makes you more memorable.

140 See 'Cerebral Lateralization of Pro- and Anti-Social Tendencies', Hecht, D., in *Experimental Neurobiology*, March 2014
141 *The Master and His Emissary*, p70

Awe.

A sense of wonder before something much greater than oneself is something that can only be appreciated by the right brain. McGilchrist explains that awe is usually experienced before nature, before depth or height, before enormity, an extraordinary event, before beauty or complexity. This type of experience both makes us feel small, as McGilchrist explains, but at the same time 'extends' the being of the beholder,[142] so that we also feel part of that moment and place. We are both separate to and connected with what we are experiencing, because, as Haidt puts it, we must "accommodate the experience by changing [our existing mental structures]". He continues, "Awe acts as a kind of mental reset button: it makes people forget themselves and their petty concerns".[143] In other words, it gives us a sense of perspective. In advertising, it is usually felt in response to executional brilliance, inviting the question, 'How did they do that?'; the sort of feeling we get when we watch Sony Bravia's *Bouncing Balls* ad.

Upliftment.

Ekman describes upliftment, referencing Jonathan Haidt's description 'elevation' as the heart-warming feeling people have when they see human kindness and compassion.[144] Altruism is bound up with right-brained empathy, as McGilchrist explains. The right brain reaches out to people without purpose or motive – the very definition of altruism. Altruism occurs between people who may never see each other again and who might never be able to reciprocate. Belvita's *Next Stop: Good Mornings* digital video ad elicits high levels of upliftment. It is set on a train with a chirpy conductor who tries to bring a smile to the faces of fed-up commuters.

Ecstasy or bliss.

A state of self-transcendent rapture,[145] as Ekman describes it, might be mapped to what McGilchrist refers to as the 'lived body',[146] where the body mediates our experience of the lived world. A feeling of ecstasy might be described as a heightened sense of consciousness in our engagement with the world around us. This relies on the right hemisphere's 'primary consciousness', as McGilchrist puts it, "relating our visceral and emotional experience to what we know about the world". Ecstasy or bliss is a type of happiness felt very strongly in response to John Lewis's Christmas ads, *Monty the Penguin* and *Buster the Boxer*.

These five types of happiness are particularly associated with business effects because they play to the unique talents of the right brain for empathy, understanding things on two levels, and its sense of connection with other people and the wider world. Activating the right brain makes people more favourably disposed towards your arguments.[147] It might be more helpful to describe advertising that works over the long term as *sponsored entertainment*, because for profit gain, you must speak to the right brain; you must entertain.

Short-term effects.

It is worth reflecting briefly on how we might predict the short-term effects of advertising, because it reveals the kind of advertising that works in the short term. For an ad to work in the short term, you need to attract the attention of those in the market for a product today or the very near future. This is achieved by eliciting an intense emotion of any kind and raising the salience of the brand – in other words, attracting the viewer's attention to it. System1's measure for predicting short-term effects rests on an ad's ability to elicit strongly an emotion of any kind and make a strong brand impression (the ability of the viewer to retain the brand). System1's 1-5 *Spike* measure takes its name from Binet and Field's chart shown in section 1, showing the short-term spikes associated with activation advertising.

The example opposite shows how this works for one of System1's clients, Camelot, across its activation ads. For Camelot, the product that is being advertised can vary hugely from week to week, depending on the lottery prize. Prizes can be a powerful source of appeal, but they can also confound analysis, so Camelot conducted their own econometric analysis to determine the same-week ROI of their activation ads, controlling for the effects of jackpot size. This was run for radio separately (an always-on activation channel) and all other channels combined (the bulk of which is TV). The relationship between the Spike measure and same-week ROI is significant and is shown in Fig 51 (correlation for non-radio +0.82, correlation for radio +0.84). Two ads are highlighted on the radio ad analysis. The ad highlighted in black was replaced following this analysis and an alternative version was made and aired (ad highlighted in red). In just days the new version was finished and put on air in place of the original, confirming the predictive power and commercial utility of the Spike score when optimising activation ads.

142 Idem. p363
143 *The Righteous Mind*, p264
144 *Emotions Revealed*, Ekman, P., Phoenix, London 2003
145 Idem.

146 *The Master and His Emissary*, p148
147 McGilchrist refers us to 'Induced lateral orientation and persuasibility', Drake, R. A and Bingham, B. R. *Brain and Cognition*, 1985

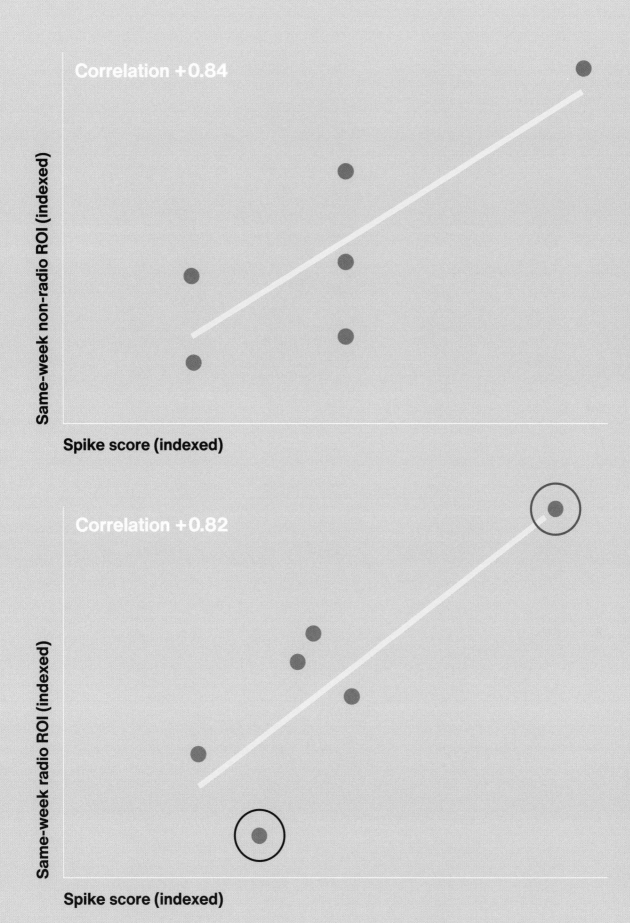

Correlation +0.84

Same-week non-radio ROI (indexed)

Spike score (indexed)

Correlation +0.82

Same-week radio ROI (indexed)

Spike score (indexed)

Fig 51 Showing the relationship between System1's short-term Spike measure and same-week ROI for non-radio ads (top) and radio ads (bottom). The line of best fit for radio shows the relationship when all ads are included.

Disruption strategy and the short term.

With budgets under pressure, advertisers have sought less expensive means to get noticed. Shock or purpose advertising can be used to 'disrupt' a category, to garner press interest and coverage, to earn media rather than pay for it. This gives a brand a moment in the spotlight; like magnesium, it burns brightly but quickly. As the Spike analysis in Fig 51 shows, advertising that elicits strong emotional response regardless of its valence (i.e. seeks to elicit a strong emotional response across a population, whether 'positive' or 'negative') is helpful in the short term. Whether seeking to shock or antagonise half of the population is helpful over the longer term, for brands or the industry, is more questionable.

The desire to disrupt or shock is a feature of modernism, is seen in schizophrenic patients and is unquestionably a left-brain instinct, as McGilchrist points out. Antonin Artaud, the French avant-garde dramatist who conceptualised the 'theatre of cruelty' and who suffered himself from schizophrenia, once said, "I wanted a theatre that would be like a shock treatment, galvanise, shock people into feeling".[148] The same instinct can be said to be behind the strategy of advertising 'disruption'. Disruption strategy is a left-brain instinct that is inherently weighted towards the short term.

Disruption advertising manifests itself in different ways, the first being the *anti-ad*, such as Old Blue Last's *Balloon for Popping, Beer for Drinking* (US) or Brew Dog's *Punk IPA* (UK) ads. The anti-ad is conceived to shock, not entertain; it is emptied out of all feeling (these two anti-ads achieve 1-Star in testing). In this respect, the anti-ad has much in common with the punk movement and any effects are likely to be short-lived. As Sir John Hegarty explains, punk "jolted conventional thinking without putting anything in its place – it created a void but failed to fill it", and "if you're going to knock something down, you have to put something in its place".[149]

The other principal kind of disruption ad is the purpose or manifesto ad. Disruptive purpose advertising tends to pitch one set of moral values against another. *Individualistic* values of care/harm and fairness/cheating tend to be pitched against *binding* values of loyalty/betrayal, authority/subversion and sanctity/degradation, as described in section 4. An example of this kind of ad would be Nike's *Dream Crazy Kaepernick* ad. This split the audience in testing, achieving a low 2-Star, suggesting only average long-term effects.[150] The intensity of emotion it elicited, however (both positive and negative), earned it a strong 4-Spike score, pointing to strong short-term response. And indeed, it did succeed in gaining a great deal of coverage. **For purpose advertising that creates strong *long-term* effects, don't seek to divide and pitch values against each other; play instead to values that everyone can agree on.** A good example of this is Always' *Like a Girl* (4-Star).

In section 3, we reflected on the lack of trust that the general public has today in advertising. In section 4, we highlighted the gap that has emerged in values between agencies and the public. Disruption strategy risks driving the wedge deeper still because a) left-brain shock tactics irritate and b) prioritising one set of values over another stokes and perpetuates division. Advertisers use shock tactics in the hope of galvanising the populace, but in so doing they run the risk of talking down to it. This will not promote trust in advertising among the public any more than in the brands it represents. To connect with the mainstream consider espousing a sense of community; they will be more receptive to it.[151] As we will see in our final section, lasting effects can be more reliably achieved by creating *human* cultural reference points.

The desire to disrupt or shock is a feature of modernism, is seen in schizophrenic patients and is unquestionably a left-brain instinct.

148 McGilchrist references *The Diary of Anais Nin: 1931-1934*, Nin, A., Swallow Press, New York 1966, for the quotation
149 *Hegarty on Advertising*, p 35

Metaphor.

Metaphors help us to understand the world. They are not simply a frivolous linguistic ornament. They imbue a context with an altogether richer meaning, more than an explicit or literal description ever could. As McGilchrist explains, "metaphors link language to life".[152] They give life and energy to ideas; they are a "vehicle for thought".[153]

"Metaphor [...] is a means whereby the truly new, rather than just the novel, may come about. When a metaphor actually lives in the mind it can generate new thoughts or understanding – it is cognitively real and active."[154]

Metaphors are therefore important in creative development, as we saw in Section 4, because they can give form to new ideas; a form that can be made to *live* in advertising. They connect with the right brain because they require an understanding of context – the relationship of one context with another. They are also intrinsically linked to humour because to appreciate humour, the right brain has to be able to see things from two perspectives and understand how context can change meaning.

There is a modern left-brain tendency to explain or labour metaphors, showing for instance an image of a fat cat next to the copy 'fat cat'. This is what McGilchrist would describe as "a dead historical remnant of a once live metaphor, a cliché".[155] Making the metaphor literal in this way is unlikely to generate a strong emotional response.

Humour, the portrayal of the living, and fresh metaphors are essential for connecting with audiences and conveying complex and new ideas quickly, simply and implicitly.

150 Subsequent ads in the 'Dream' campaign have been less divisive and have scored progressively higher
151 See *The collapse of context: Seeing through the promise of social media community building*, Tenzer, A., www.thedrum.com April 2019

152 *The Master and His Emissary*, p115
153 Idem. p332
154 Idem. p179
155 Idem. p179

Creativity for the long term: The 'fluent device'.

In section 1, we discussed the importance of processing fluency. The Ehrenberg-Bass Institute stresses the importance of distinctive assets – brand properties such as logos, fonts, shapes, colours.[156] This is because they help processing fluency, enable people to access a brand mentally and recognise it swiftly when they see it. People tend to like what they can process quickly. From an evolutionary perspective, it's less likely to be a threat because we've encountered it before, but it also reduces cognitive load. We reward anything that reduces cognitive load; we like it more and will pay more for it. Consistent use of the same asset or property is helpful for any brand, because **recognition speeds decision**. While logos, fonts, shapes, colours are very important, they are merely signs and symbols – things dealt with by the left brain, much like language. Familiarity of these things can generate positive affect over time, but there are better ways to connect with the right brain in advertising. The trick is to prioritise the *living*.[157]

We call such a vehicle a *fluent device*. A fluent device is a recurring character with agency or a recurring scenario played out by people in new and different contexts. It lives or presents the living in a context; it can be a metaphor for something the brand wishes to communicate. It gives you opportunity to entertain and, because it is rooted in characters and people, to imbue your advertising with many of the highly desirable right-brain features discussed in section 3.

We use two definitions:

The first of these definitions describes campaigns such as Comparethemarket's Meerkats (UK) or Geico's Gecko (US), the M&M's characters or indeed some of the historical advertising characters described in section 4, such as the Smash Martians, the Honey Monster or the Cresta Bear.

The second definition centres on a pay-off that can be expressed through many different (but fundamentally similar) scenarios, such as Specsavers' 'Should've gone to Specsavers', Snickers' 'You're not you when you're hungry' or even the historical Heineken campaign discussed in section 3, 'Refreshes the parts that other beers cannot reach'.

These definitions mark out fluent devices as something different from emotional storytelling ads or ads featuring more straightforward non-living distinctive assets, such as a logo or a jingle. The definitions also make clear that the fluent device should appear more than once in a campaign – so the classic John Lewis UK Christmas ads, for instance, *wouldn't count* as a fluent-device campaign, as Monty The Penguin, Moz The Monster and their other characters only ever appear once. The definitions also make clear that the fluent device should drive the story in the ad – so classic brand mascots like the Jolly Green Giant would be out, unless they were at the centre of the action.

System1 used the IPA Effectiveness Databank to test the hypothesis that *long-term campaigns with a fluent device are more likely to generate profit gain than campaigns that don't*.

1
A fictitious character or characters (humans or creatures) created by the brand and used as the primary vehicle for the drama in more than one ad across a campaign.

2
A scenario, expressed as a slogan, used more than once in a campaign as the primary vehicle for the drama without which the ad would make little sense.

156 See *How Brands Grow*, Sharp, B., Oxford University Press 2010 and *Building Distinctive Brand Assets*, Romaniuk, J., Oxford University Press 2018
157 *The Master and His Emissary*, pp55-56. See also *Building Distinctive Brand Assets*, Romaniuk pp139-142

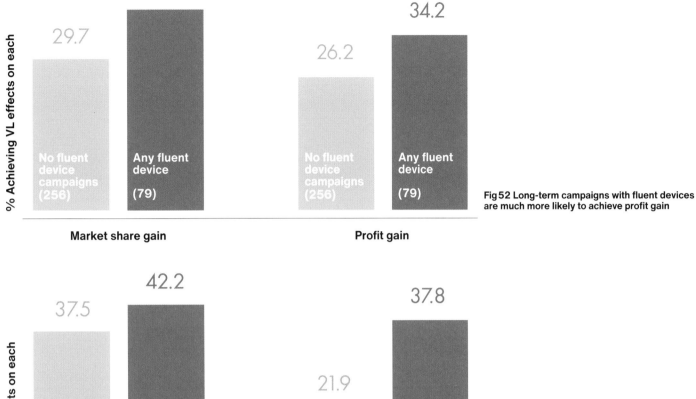

% Achieving VL effects on each

39.2

29.7

No fluent device campaigns (256)

Any fluent device (79)

Market share gain

34.2

26.2

No fluent device campaigns (256)

Any fluent device (79)

Profit gain

Fig 52 Long-term campaigns with fluent devices are much more likely to achieve profit gain

% Achieving VL effects on each

42.2

37.5

No fluent device campaigns (128)

Any fluent device (45)

Market share gain

37.8

21.9

No fluent device campaigns (128)

Any fluent device (45)

Profit gain

Fig 53 Long-term campaigns with fluent devices are more efficient over the long term

9.7   6.5   9.7   6.5   **Average ESOV**

System1 identified campaigns in the IPA Effectiveness Databank that met either definition above and those that didn't, going back to 1992. This exercise was conducted blind, without knowing the campaigns' effectiveness, to prevent bias. System1's list of tagged campaigns was then analysed by Peter Field to compare the effectiveness of long-term campaigns that used a fluent device with those that didn't.

There were over 620 long-term campaigns in the IPA Effectiveness Databank. Over 490 campaigns dated from 1992 or later. That date is important because in 1991 the IPA introduced its 'Long and Broad Effects' award, and the number of long-term campaign entries markedly increased in 1992. System1 coded up all campaigns since 1992 that employed a fluent device, but the effectiveness analysis looks at the 330 campaigns from 1999 onwards. This is when new effectiveness fields were introduced and have remained consistent since.

The analysis reveals that **campaigns with a fluent device are much more likely to achieve market share and profit gain than campaigns without.**

Long-term campaigns that use a fluent device are a third more likely to report very large business effects of market share and profit gain; using a fluent device increases your chances of achieving these major business effects. If we look at the same analysis for those campaigns declaring extra share of voice, it's clear that this isn't just a function of spend. Campaigns in the IPA Effectiveness Databank with a fluent device historically receive less support, yet they are still more effective. They give you greater long-term impact for less spend.

Both 'character' and 'scenario' based fluent devices are highly effective, but there do seem to be some slight differences in the business effects a brand can expect.

Character-based fluent devices have a better chance of winning over new customers and a slightly better chance of creating market-share gain. They also have a better chance of reducing price sensitivity – a very rare but important advertising effect that's crucial for profitability. This confirms what we know about fluency from psychological studies, which is that we confer greater value on things that are quick and easy to process.[158]

Scenario fluent devices have marginally more impact on profit gain and on short-term sales activation. Character fluent devices are highly visual, and broadly recognisable even to non-buyers, and that helps them to expand a brand's reach. A slogan fluent device meanwhile is easier for people to imitate or parody, and serves as a call to action for those people already in the market for the product (e.g. 'Should've gone to Specsavers'), which means it can achieve a cultural impact – and a sales impact – more quickly.

The fluent device speaks to the right brain, allowing you to draw on the right-brain features that are associated with greater effectiveness: a clear sense of time and place, a scene unfolding, characters with agency, implicit communication, dialogue, accents, subversion of language, the referencing of other cultural works, and music. The fluent device protects against the instincts of the left brain and prevents it from manifesting itself in your advertising. It enables you to sustain your brand consistently over a long time period. These campaigns can be sustained profitably for many, many years; the general public doesn't tire of them the way the boardroom thinks it does.

With its emphasis on repeatability and sustainability, the fluent device is the whole-brained creative solution, working with the unique faculties of the right brain, but satisfying the commercial need for consistency and repeatability required by the left.

The fluent device is the whole-brained creative solution

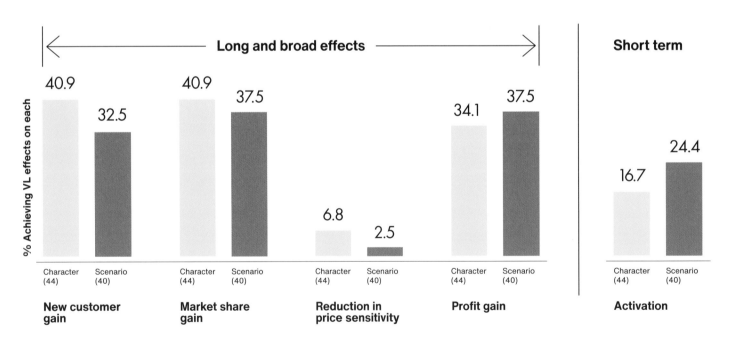

Fig 54 The effectiveness of character and scenario fluent devices

158 See *Easy on the mind, easy on the wallet: The roles of familiarity and processing fluency in valuation judgements,* Alter, A. L. & Oppenheimer, D. M., Psychonomic Bulletin & Review, 15(5), 985-990, 2008

A device worth keeping.

The cultural shift described in section 3 has also sent the fluent device into decline. Back in 1992, 41% of IPA submissions contained a fluent device. By 2016, that had fallen to 12%. The decline has been particularly dramatic since 2006. In a period when left-brain instincts dominate, metaphor, characters and place are sidelined. Yet there are very good reasons to bring them back for the digital age.

Referencing the System1 Ad Ratings database, it's possible to go beyond the IPA Effectiveness Databank to determine the prevalence of the fluent device on TV advertising in the UK and US today. System1 has reviewed a year's advertising from System1 Ad Ratings, amounting to 16,675 ads, and identified that the character fluent device features in fewer than 10% of all TV ads today in the categories covered by System1 Ad Ratings. This is in line with the findings from the IPA Effectiveness Databank. Character fluent devices are of interest to us because they are highly visual properties with the ability to make an impression quickly across platforms, as we shall see shortly.

It is possible to learn something about what makes character fluent device ads so effective, by identifying them on System1's Ad Ratings database.

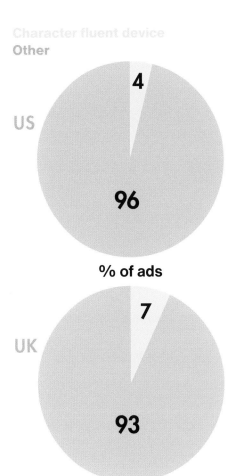

Fig 56 The prevalence of the character fluent device on TV today

Character fluent device
Other

US

4

96

% of ads

UK

7

93

% of long-term campaign submissions with character or scenario fluent device

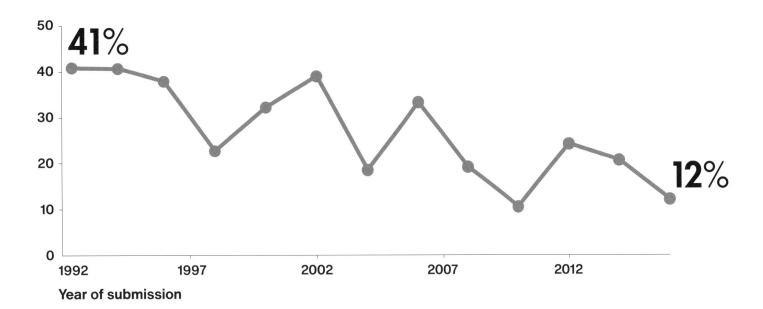

Year of submission

Fig 55 Plotting the decline in the use of fluent devices

Campaigns with a *fluent device* elicit stronger emotional response and so greater long-term growth prospects than campaigns that don't feature them.

Fluent devices also create memory structures for brand recognition, making investment go further.

Fig 56 Some of the UK's character fluent devices
Source: permissions direct from client and/or IPA Effectiveness Awards

(Did your right brain spot the 'F' for Fluency?)

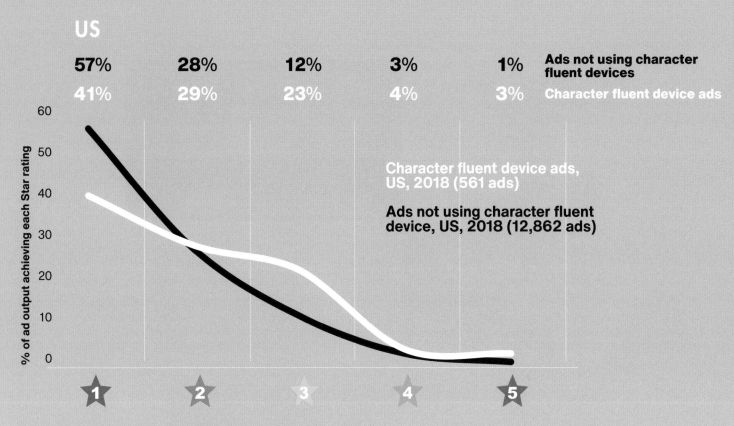

Fig 57 The emotional surplus generated by character fluent devices (US)

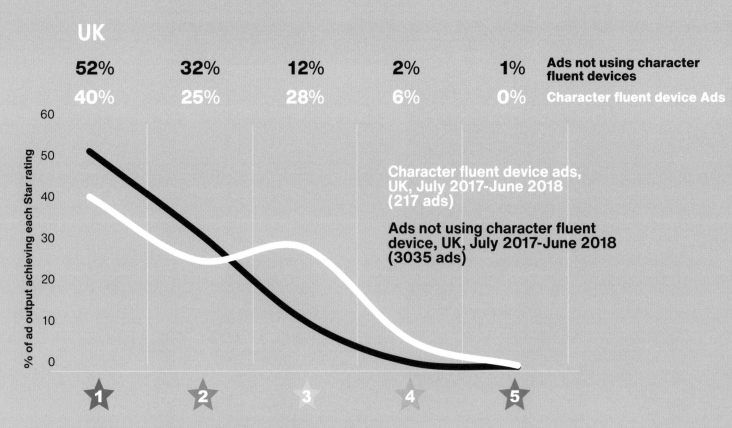

Fig 58 The emotional surplus generated by character fluent devices (UK)

In both the UK and the US, ads featuring a **fluent device enjoy stronger emotional response and therefore greater long-term growth prospects** than ads that don't feature them.

Treating each of the lines shown in the graphs opposite as a brand and running it through System1's growth model suggests that the emotional surplus that a character Fluent device develops is worth an additional 8% points of SOV in the US and an additional 12% points of SOV in the UK. **Fluent devices have a real media value.** They also build memory structures.

Fig 59 shows a comparison of TV spend and the proportion of people correctly identifying the brand on System1's database. This is shown for both ads with and without a character fluent device. The analysis reveals a positive relationship between spend and brand identification. This is to be expected, because the ads in the System1 Ad Ratings database have been post-tested. The greater the spend, the greater the chances are that people will have seen the ad more than once and the easier it will be for them to identify the brand.

What is particularly striking, however, is the relationship between spend and brand identification for ads with a character fluent device. First, there is very little brand misattribution – the lowest brand identification score is 65%; contrast this with those ads with no character fluent device. Second, the relationship between spend and brand recognition is much stronger.

TV spend

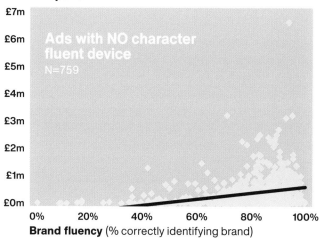

Brand fluency (% correctly identifying brand)

TV spend

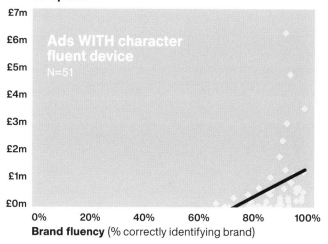

Brand fluency (% correctly identifying brand)

Fig 59 Brand recognition against spend for ads with and without a character fluent device

Fluent devices in a multi-platform world.

It is in the period since 2000 that we have witnessed the growth of online channels. Let's explore the extent to which fluent devices are being used on other channels and, in particular, digital and social channels.

Fig 61 shows the proportion of all marketing that features a character fluent device across the different channels that are used by brands with a fluent device in the UK. Only 63% of all ads on TV for brands with a fluent device feature their fluent device. This falls further for those fluent device brands using YouTube and direct mail. Here, character fluent devices only feature in 39% of all ads or mail packs. Brands use their fluent device even less on the social platforms of Facebook (24%) and Twitter (21%).

This perhaps stems from a reluctance to feature anything that *looks* like advertising on these social channels, and instead to feature 'relevant' content – recipes or lifestyle videos – because, since the early days of these channels, there has been a long-held view that advertising and brands are not welcome in social spaces. The drive for very literal left-brained 'relevant' content, often presented flat, from above, focusing on how things are made, has triumphed over the pure artifice of right-brained character advertising.

If advertisers and agencies are spurning the fluent device in digital channels, it is a major opportunity missed. Audiences have much greater control over an online advertising environment and process it at speed. In these environments, a familiar character or slogan will very quickly refresh the neural networks associated with the brand and generate an emotional response before the viewer has chance to move on to the next piece of content. It's also more likely to attract the right brain's attention.

Working with British Gas, in a split test sponsored by Newsworks, eye-tracking specialist Lumen and System1 tested two versions of a British Gas video on a high-attention and low-attention website. One version of the ad featured Wilbur the Penguin – British Gas' fluent device – the other didn't. Eye tracking reveals that more people watch the ad when the character is present, resulting in greater effective reach. It also shows that people dwell on the ad for longer and are better able to recall the brand afterwards. The ad with the Penguin scores 3 Stars, performing better than the ad without, which only achieves 2 Stars in testing. Results are shown opposite in aggregate across websites (the effect was even more marked in a high-attention news-brand context).

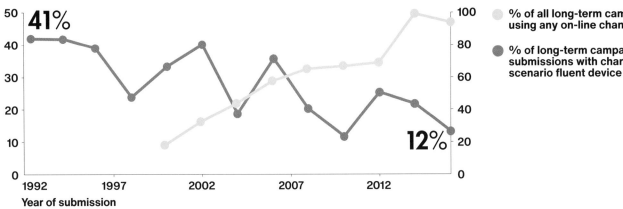

% of all long-term campaigns using any on-line channel

% of long-term campaign submissions with character or scenario fluent device

Year of submission

Fig 60 The rise in the digital channels in the period of the fluent device's decline

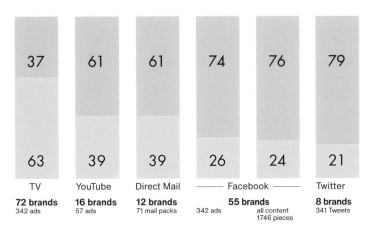

TV	YouTube	Direct Mail	Facebook		Twitter
37	61	61	74	76	79
63	39	39	26	24	21

72 brands 342 ads **16 brands** 57 ads **12 brands** 71 mail packs 342 ads **55 brands** all content 1746 pieces **8 brands** 341 Tweets

% of all ads/mail packs/content/tweets NOT featuring a fluent device

% of all ads/mail packs/content/tweets featuring a fluent device

UK

Fig 61 How fluent device brands use their fluent device across channels

Speed is the priority in online advertising, which makes processing fluency all the more important, whether it's a video ad appearing in a Facebook newsfeed, a Twitter feed or a six-second YouTube bumper. For all the talk of millennial viewers skipping TV ads, we must hold in mind that ad avoidance and skipping are cross-channel behaviours. Analysis from Lumen's eye-tracking panel shows that **only 18% of people actually see digital display ads that are technically viewable and that the average dwell time is 1.2 seconds**.[159] Many of these impressions will be experienced on mute. When audiences only partially see advertising, its effectiveness is limited, as Professor Karen Nelson-Field has shown.[160] All of which means that with digital video, **you don't have long to make an impression**. A character fluent device will mitigate against a viewer skipping past your ad and help to create a brand impression.

Part of what makes things easy to process and recognise is congruence – a feeling of natural fit between content and its context. The timeliness of successful Tweets, like Oreo's famous 'Super Bowl blackout' tweet, makes use of this aspect of fluency. Fluent devices are a natural fit with social media because they're rooted in characters or scenarios with a well-known expression. When the Philadelphia Eagles won the 2018 Super Bowl, Bud Light could quickly switch

its 'Dilly Dilly' catchphrase for 'Philly Philly' – the right brain playing with language to reveal the new in the familiar. Memes are the *lingua franca* of internet culture and share much in common with the fluent device.

Fluent devices are, then, a perfect fit with the modern media world brands find themselves in and give digital platforms an opportunity to contribute to a client's long-term growth ambitions. Character fluent devices can be used in all kinds of brand experiences or customer exchanges to make them more memorable and distinctive. They can also be a source of pride for employees. Advertisers who embrace the idea of the fluent device will make online platforms work harder for them over the long term. Fluent devices – both characters and slogans – work because people like them. They are entertaining, human, part of pop culture, and proud of it. They matter for brands because they are effective. They matter for the industry because of the regard that society holds them in, for the levels of trust they engender and, in turn, for the talent that it attracts. They matter for the economy and they matter for society, because they are cultural beacons, common reference points, part of the fabric of popular culture. **They are the cultural glue that holds us together; it's our responsibility that this glue doesn't become unstuck.**

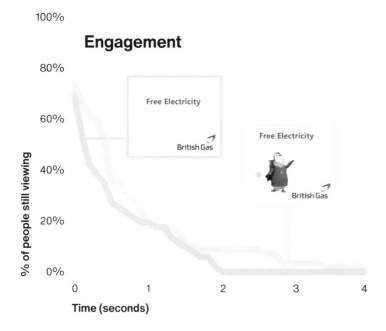

Fig 62 The increased benefits for reach, dwell time and brand recall for an ad with a character fluent device

	Free Electricity British Gas	Free Electricity British Gas
% Viewing (effective reach)	69	74
Average dwell time (seconds)	0.6	0.9
% Spontaneous brand recall	28	35

159 See *Context Enhances Attention and Grows Sales*, Follett, M. Lumen use the IAB definition of viewability: at least 50% of its pixels are available to be seen for one second or more
160 See *How much should media Cost? An analysis of CPM's and impact across TV, Facebook and YouTube in Australia*, Nelson-Field, Riebe and Banelis 2018

Section 5
Summary.

1 For profit gain, speak to the right brain. Broad and long-term effects are associated with advertising that elicits happiness, that amuses, that leaves people awestruck, that plays to a connection with other people and the wider world. All the evidence shows that most advertising isn't fun anymore, and that is, in no small part, why effectiveness is declining.

2 Short-term effects can be achieved by generating intense emotional response in the viewer regardless of valence ('positive' and 'negative' emotional response), but this is no guarantee of long-term effects.

3 What burns brightly, burns quickly. The desire to 'disrupt' in advertising is a left-brain instinct; the desire to shock and polarise opinion is a strategy geared towards the short-term.

4 Metaphor in the form of repeatable characters and human scenarios is a means of generating and sustaining growth over the long term. We call this the *fluent device.*

5 Fluent devices work as a particularly powerful kind of distinctive asset. They are powerful because they engage the right brain, with its pre-occupation for the *living*. Distinctive assets such as logos, shapes and fonts all help to create processing fluency, but living things get noticed by the right brain and entertain it.

6 There has been a decline in the use of the fluent device since the advent of online channels. This is a missed opportunity because characters get advertising noticed and watched in digital contexts, helping brands who want to use these platforms for sustained growth over the long term.

7 Relevance is not enough. For growth, you must make people *feel more*: entertain for commercial gain.

Conclusions.

1 Advertising is a force for good, but this century has seen a decline in advertising creativity. This is harming advertising's ability to connect with audiences and is reducing its effectiveness.

2 The features that made it effective have been lost; the features that hinder effectiveness have become more commonplace. Since 2006, advertising has become flat, abstracted, dislocated and devitalised, and overly reliant on the 'word'. It has lost its humanity – the use of metaphor, characters, dialogue and betweenness – and it has become dislocated from its time and place. This is harming its ability to elicit an emotional response in audiences, which is essential for long-term growth and profitability.

3 Understanding how the brain works can help us to explain what has happened and how to make things better. New and painstaking work by neuropsychologist Iain McGilchrist reveals the preferred attentional styles of the left and right brains. The left brain is analytical and literal, it prizes repetition, it is goal oriented, it abstracts things from their context, creating flat models of the world and tools to manipulate it; the right brain sees the whole and the relationships between things, it understands depth and perspective, lived time, music, and is alert to novelty, metaphor, humour and the living.

4 Advertising reflects, but it also shapes culture. This change in advertising style is one strand of a broader shift in culture and it is possible to trace such shifts in the past. We are living in a time of left-brain dominance and advertising today is betraying the left brain's preferences.

5 We propose that many cultural factors have got us here, stemming from the industry's more left-brain instincts. Clients have shortened timeframes for creative development and adopted short-term measures of return. Creative control is very centralised in client companies today. Agency remuneration has come under downward pressure from procurement departments, who have also introduced centralised processes that break up the creative task into smaller parts. Holding companies have introduced productivity drives in agencies that reduce headcounts and increase workloads. They have also encouraged specialism, which is not conducive to creativity, and worked with clients to promote the global ad. Digital platforms are issuing guidelines that encourage short spots, abstraction and rhythm. Those working in advertising, media and marketing today have a highly analytical, rather than holistic, thinking style. The attentional preferences of the left brain are also responsible for short-termism and ever-tighter targeting.

6 Advertising works over the long term by entertaining people and sustaining their enjoyment, not by seeking to shock and divide. This demands the unique talents of the right brain. The right brain works best with conversational briefing. In creative development, it's important to build on an idea, to go with the flow, not to reduce or abstract it. Creative development is a craft, not a profession, and requires you to put something of yourself into it. An ad can be made better at every stage (the script is not a legal document) and the right kind of research can help to make advertising ideas better. Make the most of the instincts of actors and directors, and embrace the happy accident along the way; this takes an ad from ordinary to extraordinary. Use music early in the briefing process – it can *give form* to the idea, it helps you to connect, convey meaning and signal the brand. Finally, embrace the living in characters, scenarios and metaphor – the *fluent device* – to entertain your audience. Advertising must entertain for commercial gain.

Implications.

With effectiveness on the slide, there is a real opportunity
to do advertising differently and better. If we were drawing up
a manifesto for a new agency today, what might it look like,
given all that we have learned?

Agency manifesto

We are an agency that always has an eye on the long term in our work and
measurement; we prioritise clients' future customer base and work to reduce price
sensitivity towards your brand. Profitable growth requires people to *feel more*. We
seek to entertain for commercial gain, not to shock or disrupt. This is the fastest
and surest route to increased profits. This guides our beliefs and practices:

1   We believe that advertising is a craft, not a profession; we want you to know
    that it takes talent and time to create extraordinary work.

2   We write for the public rather than the judges; our employees are attuned to
    what people like.

3   We are known for our memorable characters and human situations, which the
    public loves and talks about. Your employees will love them too.

4   We believe in local – rather than global – work, because local work is more
    effective. It will cost you more, but you will get more back.

5   We believe that creative businesses and their reputations are built on their
    work, which in turn attracts the best talent. Our management understands that
    the value we bring lies in our craft, not our productivity.

6   We believe in keeping left-brain processes away from our creatives.
    These stifle creativity.

7   We follow right-brain working methods all the way through from briefing to
    production; when you see our script, know that it is only the start point, not the
    destination.

8   We believe in fostering lasting partnerships between our creatives. Multiple
    teams working on one brief, specialism and 'hot-team' approaches may be fine
    for technology 'sprints' but are no basis for sustaining brands over the
    long term.

9   Research, done correctly, enables you to see that our work is connecting with
    your audience. Our creatives believe in it as a guide.

10 We love technology and awe-inspiring visual effects, but we believe people,
    betweenness, time, place, music, metaphor and humour, are at the heart of
    great advertising.

Who wouldn't want to buy from that agency?

Epilogue.

Narrowness of focus and short-termism are the instincts of a dominant left brain; today's flatness, abstraction and devitalisation are features of it.

Advertising relies on the instincts of the right brain to connect with its audiences, but the left brain has taken control. The left brain has many qualities that improve the human condition. It's just that it tends to overreach itself sometimes, to overwhelm its silent intuitive partner. Its overconfidence is misplaced; it lacks empathy, a sense of the living and it understands the world only through its own distorting prism. Creativity and originality require both left and right hemispheres to operate in tandem. Both are important for leaps of greatness. But somewhere along the line, the master has become a slave to its servant. We are today in a period of left-brain dominance; a strained, brittle and curiously flat period, a creative *Reformation.*

A creative director, reflecting recently on what had changed over the years, told me, "it's just not fun anymore". A rush towards processes, a squeeze on resources, an increase in workload all have a habit of stifling creativity. As de Toqueville might have put it, a "network of small complicated rules" has emerged "through which the most original minds and the most energetic characters cannot penetrate".[161]

Nothing stays the same forever, however, and it is hoped that this volume points to a brighter future.

Advertising needs to entertain for commercial gain. When it doesn't, the whole advertising ecosystem runs to seed; when it does, it unlocks growth and builds reputations.

This publication has described how the advertising brain turned sour – how advertising has lost its humanity and betweenness – and suggested how we might make things *right* again. It has pointed to the type of advertising that moves people, and the company culture and working practices that are needed to create it. It describes what creativity in the service of long-term growth looks like. It also demonstrates the value of research; how it provides both confidence and guidance.

Connecting with audiences requires us to connect with their right brain. This can only be achieved by freeing our own right brain. In creative development, we must resist our instincts to analyse and devitalise. "What is important now is to recover our senses. We must learn to see more, to hear more, to feel more."[162]

The future of advertising depends upon it.

" **Agencies and their clients need to recapture some of the respect, fun and profitability of working in what was once one of the most fulfilling and glamorous of industries but has become a grim sweatshop for the people who do the work.** "

Michael Farmer

161 *Democracy in America,* trans. Reeve, H. & Plaag, E. W., Barnes and Noble, New York, 2003, pp723-4, as referenced by McGilchrist, *The Master and His Emissary*, p346
162 *Against Interpretation*, Sontag, S. 1964

Acknowledgments.

I would like to thank Janet Hull OBE and the IPA for supporting this publication.

I would also like to thank Dr Iain McGilchrist for the support and guidance he has given me while I wrote it, for his permission to reprint images in his book and to reference him liberally.

I would like to thank Adrian Holmes and John O'Driscoll for the front cover, who willingly gave their time and talent to create it.

I would like to thank Les Binet, David Buttle, Sarah Carter, Paul Feldwick, Peter Field, Simon Gill, Laurence Green, Sophie Grender, Matt Hill, Adrian Holmes, Margaret Jobling, Jon Lombardo, David Meikle, John O'Driscoll, Seamus O'Farrell, Ian Pring, Rory Sutherland, Andrew Tenzer, Sue Unerman, Charles Vallance and Jon Webb for their support and input, all of whom have helped to make this a better publication.

I would like to thank Thinkbox, Nielsen (Ebiquity), Numerator, Figure8 and Picasso Labs for providing me with the wherewithal to conduct the analysis.

I would like to thank Hazel Collier and Sinead Mead at Camelot for their analysis of our Spike measure in relation to their own econometric analysis, and for Camelot's permission to publish here.

I would like to thank Professor Søren Handberg of Oslo University and Professor Siri Sande for their help in tracking down the Roman images in section 2.

I would like to thank Colin Morris for allowing me to reproduce his analysis of pop music lyrics in section 3.

I would like to thank Karen Fraser, Credos and the Advertising Association for allowing me to reproduce their analysis of favourability towards advertising in section 3.

I would like to thank Grant Morrison of Morrison Dalley for designing this book.

Finally, I would like to thank System1 for allowing me the time to write the book, and the help and support of my colleagues, in particular John Kearon, Tom Ewing, Will Headley, Will Goodhand, Colin Jenkinson and Bruce Bickerton. I'd also like to thank Alice Meehan for her help with the analysis.

Bibliography.

Abernathy, W.J., Wayne, K., 'Limits of the Learning Curve', *Harvard Business Review*, September, 1974

Alter, A. L. & Oppenheimer, D.M., 'Easy on the mind, easy on the wallet: The roles of familiarity and processing fluency in valuation judgements', *Psychonomic Bulletin & Review,* 15(5), pp985-990, 2008

Angear, B., *Advertising Works 23*: IPA Effectiveness Awards, WARC, London, 2016

Binet, L. and Field, P., *Effectiveness in Context; A Manual for Brand Building*, IPA, London, 2018

Binet, L. and Field, P., *The Long and the Short of It,* IPA, London, 2013

Binet, L. and Field, P., *Marketing in the Era of Accountability*, IPA, 2008

Binet, L. and Field, P., *Media in Focus*, IPA, 2017

Boyd, M., *Bach*, from *The Master Musicians* series, J. M. Dent & Sons, London, 1983

Carter, S., *John Webster. The Earth People's Ad Man*, DDB UK Limited, London, 2012

Carter, S., 'John Webster: A creative legend's lessons for planners', *AdMap*, February, 2013

Carter, S., 'Timeless lessons for planners', *AdMap*, April, 2014

Cassidy, F., *The Board-Brand Rift*, Financial Times in partnership with the IPA, 2019

Cobban, A., *The Eighteenth Century*, Thames and Hudson, London, 1969

Damasio, A., *Descartes' Error*, Vintage, London, 2006

Epstein, D., *Range*, Macmillan, London, 2019

Ekman, P., *Emotions Revealed*, Phoenix (Orion Books), London, 2004

Farmer, M., *Madison Avenue Manslaughter*, LID Publishing, London, 2019

Feldwick, P., *The Anatomy of Humbug*, Matador, Kibworth Beauchamp, 2015

Feldwick, P., 'A True Story: The Birth of a Great Campaign', Paul Feldwick, in *Market Leader*, Issue 31, Winter 2005

Field, P., *Selling Creativity Short*, IPA, 2016

Field, P., *The Crisis in Creative Effectiveness*, IPA, 2019

Follett, M., *Context Enhances Attention and Grows Sales*, AdMap, July 2018

Garland, H.&M., *The Oxford Companion to German Literature*, Oxford University Press, 1991

Godber, N., *Advertising Works 24*: IPA Effectiveness Awards WARC, London, 2018

Grave, J., *Caspar David Friedrich*, Prestel Publishing Ltd., London, 2017

Haidt, J., *The Righteous Mind*, Penguin Books, London, 2013

Hay, D., *The Age of the Renaissance*, Thames and Hudson, London, 1967

Hecht, D., 'Cerebral Lateralization of Pro- and Anti-Social Tendencies', *Experimental Neurobiology*, March 2014, 23(1), pp1-27

Hegarty, J. Sir, *Hegarty on Advertising*, Thames and Hudson, London, 2017

Hilmar, E., *Franz Schubert In His Time*, Amadeus Press, Portland, 1985

Himes, G., 'Surf Music' from teachrock.org. from *Rock and Roll: An American History*, date unknown

Kahneman, D., *Thinking Fast and Slow*, Penguin Books, 2012

Kearon, J., Ewing, T., Wood, O., *System1: Unlocking Profitable Growth*, System1 Group, 2017

Koerner, J.,L., *The Reformation of the Image*, University of Chicago Press, Chicago, 2008

L'Orange, H.P., *Art Forms and Civic Life in the Late Roman Empire*, Princeton University Press, New Jersey, 1972

Ling, R., *Roman Painting*, Cambridge University Press, 1991

McGilchrist, I., *The Master and His Emissary*, Yale University Press, New Haven and London, 2019

Munro, E.C., Rudorff, R., *Art Treasures of the World*, Hamlyn Publishing Group, London, 1970

Nelson-Field, K., Riebe, E., Banelis, M., *How much should media cost? An analysis of CPM's and impact across TV, Facebook and YouTube in Australia*, Centre for Amplified Intelligence, August 2018

Nikolaenko, N. N., Egorov, A. Y. & Freiman, A. E., 'Representation activity of the right and left hemispheres of the brain', *Behavioural Neurology*, 1997, 10(1), pp49-59

Prawer, S.S., *The Penguin Book of Lieder*, Penguin Books Limited, 1964

Price, G., *Thinklong: I believe the future of brands requires collective action to combat short-termism*, WARC, 2018

Romaniuk, J., *Building Distinctive Brand Assets*, Oxford University Press, Melbourne, 2018

Sadie, S., Latham, A., *The Cambridge Music Guide*, Cambridge University Press, 1990

Sharp, B., *How Brands Grow*, Oxford University Press, 2010

Sontag, S., *Against Interpretation*, 1964

Taylor, A. and Greve, H. R., 'Superman or Fantastic Four? Knowledge Combination and Experience in Innovative Teams', *Academy of Management Journal* 49, no.4 (2006): pp723-40

Tenzer, A. and Murray, I., *Why We Shouldn't Trust Our Gut Instinct*, Reach Solutions/House51 whitepaper, 2018

Tenzer, A., and Murray, I, *The Empathy Delusion*, Reach Solutions/House51 whitepaper, 2019

Serrà, J., Corral, A., Boguñá, M., Haro, M. and Arcos, J.L., 'Measuring the Evolution of Contemporary Western Popular Music', *Scientific Reports* volume 2, Article number: 521 (2012)

Trott, D., 'Efficiency v Effectiveness', *Campaign Magazine*, May 16 2019

Wood, O., 'How Emotional Tugs Trump Rational Persuasion', *Journal of Advertising Research*, 2012

Websites.

Advertising Association and Deloitte, *Advertising Pays 1*, 2013
https://www.adassoc.org.uk/credos-category/ad-pays/

Agency Remuneration, IPA, ISBA, MAA and PRCA, 2012
http://www.thegoodpitch.com/wp-content/uploads/2012/01/Agency-Remuneration-2012.pdf

Beasley, K., 'How Agencies Are Putting Themselves Out Of Business And What We Should Do About It', *Forbes*, Jan 31 2016
https://www.forbes.com/sites/keenanbeasley/2016/01/31/how-agencies-are-putting-themselves-out-of-business-and-what-we-should-do-about-it/#282a67a549ef

www.barb.co.uk

Campbell, R. and Weigel, M., *Why Your Strategy Needs More Chaos*, Cannes Lions 2019,
https://www.youtube.com/watch?v=g63Fs6CQB8Q&app=desktop www.comedy.co.uk

Data Team, 'Why it is closing time for so many London pubs', *The Economist*, July 2017
https://www.economist.com/graphic-detail/2017/07/10/why-it-is-closing-time-for-so-many-london-pubs

Dye, D., *Stuff from the Loft*,
An interview with Sir Frank Lowe, 2019
https://davedye.com/

Dye, D., *Stuff from the Loft*,
An interview with Adrian Holmes, 2019
https://davedye.com/

Gill, R., *Master Investor*, 2016
https://masterinvestor.co.uk/equities/pump-up-your-portfolio-with-the-gym-group/

Haven, C., 'My music is better because I work harder':
Bach's St. Matthew Passion, The Book Haven blog,
Stanford University, March 2013
http://bookhaven.stanford.edu/tag/yehudi-menuhin/

Johnson, B., 'State of the agency world: Digital rules, growth slows, consultancies surge', AdAge, April 30, 2018
https://adage.com/article/agency-news/agency-report-2018/313257

Johnson, G., *Der Jüngling an der Quelle*, Hyperion, 1995,
https://www.hyperion-records.co.uk/dw.asp?dc=W1955_GBAJY0231507

Morris, C., *Are Pop Lyrics Getting More Repetitive?*
The Pudding, 2017
https://pudding.cool/2017/05/song-repetition/

Sterling, B., 'Scenius, or Communal Genius', *Wired*, 2008
https://www.wired.com/2008/06/scenius-or-comm/

Picture credits.

I would like to thank Iain McGilchrist for allowing me to reprint the Nikolaenko images (illustrations 2 and 3) from *The Master and his Emissary.*

I would like to thank Professor Sande for her permission to reproduce illustration 4 from 'Greek and Roman portraits in Norwegian Collections' from *Acta ad archaeologiam et artium historiam pertinentia*, Vol. 10, Giorgio Bretschneider, Rome, 1991. I would also like to thank her for helping me to locate illustrations 5 and 7.

I would like to thank the German Archaeological Institute in Rome for allowing the reproduction of illustration 5 and Daria Lanzuolo for helping me to source it.

I would like to thank The Norwegian Institute, Rome, University of Oslo Photographic Archive, for allowing the reproduction of illustrations 4 and 7 and Manuela Michelloni for helping me to source them.

I would also like to thank the Collection of the Duke of Northumberland, Syon House, for giving me permission to reproduce illustrations 21 and 22 from their collection.

Illustration 1 *The Divided Brain*, watercolour illustration by Orlando Wood
Illustrations 2 and 3 from Nikolaenko (1997), reproduced here from *The Master and His Emissary,* with permission from Iain McGilchrist
Illustration 4 *Portrait Bust of Decius*, Private Collection Image courtesy of Professor Sande at The Norwegian Institute, Rome, University of Oslo Photographic Archive
Illustration 5 *Bust from the Late Tetrarchy*, Museo Chiaramonti, The Vatican
Source: German Archaeological Museum, Rome
Illustration 6 *Spiral Tendrils, Ara Pacis Augustae*, Rome
Source: Foto in Comune, Musei in Comune, Sovrintendenza Capitolina, Rome
Illustration 7 *Early Medieval Spiral Tendrils*,
Santa Sabina, Rome
Source: The Norwegian Institute, Rome, University of Oslo Photographic Archive
Illustration 8 *Oplontis, Villa of Poppaei*, Pompeii
Source: Historic Images /Alamy Images
Illustration 9 *Roman Villa at Lullingstone*, British Museum
Source: British Museum Images
Illustration 10 *Procession of Figures, Ara Pacis*, Rome
Source: Historic Images/Alamy Images
Illustration 11 *Procession of Figures, Saint 'Apollinaire*, Ravenna
Source: Historic Images/Alamy Images
Illustration 12 *Scene from New Comedy*, Pompeii
Source: Historic Images /Alamy Images
Illustration 13 *The Image of Christ*, British Museum
Source: British Museum Images
Illustration 14 *Bishop Blessing the Fair at Lendit near St Denis*, Bibliothèque Nationale, Paris
Source: Historic Images /Alamy Images
Illustration 15 *Adoration of the Shepherds*, Sassetti Chapel, Santa Trinità, Florence
Source: Historic Images /Alamy Images
Illustration 16 *The Marriage of the Virgin*, Pinacoteca di Brera, Milan
Source: AKG Images
Illustration 17 *Allegory of the Old and New Testaments*, Hans Holbein the Younger, 1530, National Gallery of Scotland, Edinburgh, Scotland
Source: Historic Images/Alamy Images

Illustration 18 *The Confession of Augsburg*, Town Hall, Bad Windsheim, Germany
Source: AKG Images
Illustration 19 *Augsburg Confession*, St Johanneskirche, Schweinfurt
Source: AKG Images
Illustration 20 *Sachs portraited by Herneisen*
Source: AKG Images
Illustrations 21 and 22 *King Henry VII and Queen Elizabeth*
Source: Collection of the Duke of Northumberland, Syon Park
Illustration 23 *Coin of Friedrich the Wise*
Source: Historic Images/Alamy Images
Illustration 24 *Grand Canal Looking Northeast from the Palazzo Balbi to the Rialto Bridge*, Museo del Settecento Veneziano
Source: Scala Archives
Illustration 25 *Grand staircase of Der Residenz*, Wurzburg
Source: Historic Images /Alamy Images
Illustration 26 *Allegory on the Revolution*
Source: Historic Images /Alamy Images
Illustration 27 *Moon Rising Over the Sea*
Source: Historic Images /Alamy Images
Illustration 28 *Giant Mountains*
Source: Historic Images /Alamy Images
Illustration 29 *Wanderer above the Sea of Fog*
Source: Historic Images /Alamy Images
Illustration 30 *Interior with a girl drawing*, MOMA, New York, USA
Source: Historic Images /Alamy Images
Illustration 31 *Le Port*
Source: Historic Images /Alamy Images
'Art in the brain' illustration page 3 by Orlando Wood and Colin Jenkinson, featuring Mondrian's *Composition with Grey and Light Brown*, 1918, and Caspar David Friedrich's *Moon Rising Over the Sea*, 1821
Source: both Historic Images /Alamy Images

Index.

About the author

Orlando Wood is Chief Innovation Officer of System1 Group and member of the IPA Effectiveness Advisory Board. Co-author of *System1: Unlocking Profitable Growth* (2017), his research on advertising effectiveness draws on psychology and how the brain works.

His work has influenced thinking and practice in research, marketing and advertising, winning him awards from the ARF (Great Minds Distinction Award), the AMA (4 under 40), Jay Chiat (Gold Award for Research Innovation), ISBA (Ad Effectiveness Award), MRS (Best Paper and Research Effectiveness Awards) and ESOMAR (Best Methodology). Orlando led the IPA's Creativity and Effectiveness research for Effectiveness Week in 2018 and 2019. He has repeatedly worked with Peter Field and the IPA Effectiveness Databank to demonstrate the long and broad effects achieved by emotional advertising, most recently looking at the performance of *fluent devices*, a term he coined in work that was presented at EffWeek 2017 and 2018.

Orlando is a frequent conference speaker and has been published in *The Journal of Advertising Research, Admap* and *Market Leader*. When he's not thinking about advertising, Orlando is a semi-proficient pianist and a keen watercolour artist.

About the IPA and EffWorks

Incorporated by Royal Charter, the IPA's role is to advance the value, theory and practice of advertising, media and marketing communications; to promote best practice standards in these fields; and to ensure that the work it does will benefit the public, the wider business community and the national economy.

EffWorks is a cross-industry, long-term, global marketing-effectiveness initiative established by the IPA. Its ambition is to firmly position marketing as a route to profitable growth. It addresses the issues that impact on effectiveness and challenges the content and context of marketing outputs. Facilitated by the IPA, EffWorks creates thought leadership for the industry globally and an annual debating forum each October at Effectiveness Week London.